MW00330766

Praise for Gordon Leidner

"As the nation observes the 150th anniversary of the Civil War, the publication of this toothsome smorgasbord of memorable, revealing quotes from participants in that conflict is especially welcome. Gordon Leidner has judiciously chosen pithy statements by a wide variety of both Union and Confederate generals, common soldiers, political leaders, diarists, legislators, and commentators. It is a worthy companion to Leidner's previous collection, *Abraham Lincoln: Quotes, Quips, and Speeches*."

—*Michael Burlingame, Chancellor Naomi B. Lynn Distinguished Chair in Lincoln Studies, University of Illinois at Springfield*

"In Leidner's *The Civil War: Voices of Hope, Sacrifice, and Courage*, one finds a lucid portrayal of the key terms, issues, debates, and concerns that provoked America's greatest crisis: a civil war that would determine the future of American slavery, and therewith the future of freedom in the modern world. To read the words of the diverse array of Americans contained herein is to reflect upon the abiding challenge of self-government, and to pay the highest respect to the tragic efforts of a generation of men and women fighting for the meaning of America."

—*Lucas Morel, Head, Politics Department,*
Washington and Lee University

"The American Civil War lifted every level in American culture, from its music to the agony of its losses. It had the same effect on American words, and Gordon Leidner's handy compendium of Civil War quotes captures as none else does in its short compass the color, vehemence, sorrow, and triumph of that defining event in our history."

—*Allen C. Guelzo, Henry R. Luce Professor*
of the Civil War Era and Director, Civil War
Era Studies Program, Gettysburg College

The
CIVIL WAR

Voices OF *Hope, Sacrifice,* AND *Courage*

GORDON LEIDNER
Editor

CUMBERLAND HOUSE

Published by Cumberland House, an imprint of Sourcebooks, Inc.
P.O. Box 4410, Naperville, Illinois 60567-4410
(630) 961-3900
Fax: (630) 961-2168
www.sourcebooks.com

Library of Congress Cataloging-in-Publication data is on file with the publisher.

Printed and bound in the United States of America.
WOZ 10 9 8 7 6 5 4 3 2 1

Dedicated to my great-grandfather:
Private Philip Heinrich Leidner, Company A,
5th Missouri Regiment, USRC
Veteran of the American Civil War

Contents

Preface   ix
Introduction to the Civil War   xiii
  1 Distant Drums   1
  2 Call to Arms   21
  3 A Resolve to Win   37
  4 Character   53
  5 War Is Hell   69
  6 Facing the Inevitable   87
  7 We Are All Americans   101
Excerpts from Jefferson Davis's
  Inaugural Address   115
Excerpts from Abraham Lincoln's
  First Inaugural Address   121
The Gettysburg Address: Abraham Lincoln   127
Abraham Lincoln's Second
  Inaugural Address   131
Grant's Terms of Surrender to Lee
  at Appomattox   135
Farewell Address: General Robert E. Lee   137
Endnotes   139
About the Editor   156

"The struggle of today, is not altogether for today—it is for a vast future also."[1]

—*Abraham Lincoln*

cant

Preface

THERE IS NO saga of American history that contains more stories of hope, courage, resolve, love, and sacrifice than the American Civil War. *The Civil War: Voices of Hope, Sacrifice, and Courage* tells the story of this great conflict through the words of the men and women who experienced it firsthand. Within are quotations from presidents Abraham Lincoln and Jefferson Davis, which provide insight into the reasons for the war. The words of military leaders such as Robert E. Lee, Ulysses S. Grant, Stonewall Jackson, and William Tecumseh Sherman demonstrate not only military acumen, but also a thorough understanding of human nature. Excerpts from the diaries of women such as Mary Boykin Chesnut and Sarah Morgan Dawson tell of the civilians' hardships in war. Stories of wounded soldiers are recounted by nurses such as Clara Barton and Louisa May Alcott, revealing the heroism of both the teller and the reteller. Abolitionists such as John Brown and Henry Ward Beecher attack the injustice of slavery, while slave owners like William Lowndes Yancey and Edmund Ruffin defend it. Personal stories from former slaves such as Frederick Douglass and Harriet Tubman provide insight into the meaning of freedom, while soldiers of all ranks, Union and Confederate, convey both the horror and grandeur of war.

The Civil War abounds with some of the most enduring speeches of American history. The Gettysburg Address, Lincoln's Second Inaugural Address, and Lee's Farewell are among those included at the end of the book.

Each chapter begins with a short introduction that provides some context for the quotes that follow. To improve the quotes' readability, minor changes were occasionally made to correct capitalization, spelling, and punctuation errors. A sincere effort was made to ensure that the quotes are historically accurate, as evidenced by the endnotes in the back of the book.

Rather than attempting to trace the progress of a soldier's rank through the war, officers are usually referred to by their highest rank attained. Instead of trying to differentiate between Brigadier, Major, and Lieutenant General, all men of general rank are referred to as simply "General."

For the most part, the quotes are presented in a chronological manner. The primary purpose, however, was to arrange the quotes topically, so succeeding chapters will occasionally have a few quotes that occurred earlier in the war.

I trust that the reader will find these quotes inspirational as well as informative. I agree with many others that one cannot fully understand the United States of America today without understanding the experiences of Americans during our nation's most devastating war.

—*Gordon Leidner*

Introduction to the Civil War

Most twenty-first-century readers are amazed that it required a horrendous war, resulting in the death of hundreds of thousands of Americans, to put an end to an institution as reprehensible as slavery. It becomes even more amazing when one realizes that the majority of the Americans who fought in the Civil War did not join the army in order to either explicitly defend or eliminate slavery.

To most Southerners, the war was about preserving their "way of life" rather than preserving slavery. The majority of the Southern people had grown to accept slavery as fundamental to the South's economic survival, and their consciences had been eased regarding the "peculiar institution" by not only their political leaders, but also their religious leaders. Preachers in the

South, and sometimes in the North too, had extolled passages of the Bible supporting slavery. These religious leaders didn't bother with clarifying details such as the fact that a "slave" in the Bible would have been more accurately described as a "bond servant" in the nineteenth century. Whereas bond servants were often skilled workers who had rights such as the ability to buy their freedom, the Southern slaves had no rights and were typically slaves for life.

It was a comparative minority of Southerners, namely the slave-owning planter class, who had an overriding interest in propagating the institution of slavery. This minority had an enormous influence on the rest of their society and convinced the majority of Southerners that any threat to slavery was a threat to them all.

To most Northerners, the war was initially about preserving democratic government. Only a minority of Northerners, primarily the abolitionists, were adamant about immediately eliminating the institution of slavery. Most Northerners had never even *seen* a slave and assumed that it was only by letting the institution continue undisturbed in the South that they would avert a terrible war. They believed what the Founding Fathers had assured them—that slavery would eventually die a "peaceful death" in the South for both political and economic reasons.

But three significant events took place in the 1850s that disrupted the nation's apathy toward slavery. These were the Kansas–Nebraska Act of 1854, the Supreme Court's Dred Scott decision of 1857, and John Brown's attempted slave insurrection in 1859. The Kansas–Nebraska Act allowed settlers in new territories to determine through popular sovereignty whether they would permit slavery, negating the old Missouri Compromise that had excluded slavery in most of the new territories. The Dred Scott decision declared that people of African descent could not be American citizens and consequently had no right to sue for freedom. John Brown attempted to incite a slave revolt in Northern Virginia and was publicly hanged for his "crime."

These events triggered alarm in both the

North and the South. Northerners such as Abraham Lincoln started to believe that slavery would not die peacefully after all. They feared that it would propagate in the Western Territories and spread into Central America, becoming a permanent institution. Consequently, the North's Republican Party became adamant about preventing the spread of slavery into the new territories. Southerners such as Jefferson Davis feared that the North was going to force an end to slavery, upset the political balance of power that the South had enjoyed thus far in Congress, and destroy their agrarian way of life.

Both the Southern slave owners and Northern abolitionists took advantage of these fears. The Southern planters had, proportionately, a greater influence with the Southern people than the Northern abolitionists had with theirs. Consequently, they used this influence to initiate state conventions to consider secession from the Union. One by one, beginning with South Carolina in December 1860, these conventions voted for independence, finally resulting in eleven Southern states binding together to declare themselves a new country—the Confederate States of America. It was this declaration of Southern independence, and its consequent threat to the perpetuation of the United States, that motivated the North to arms.

The Southern slave owners had significant influence on the formation of the Constitution of the Confederate States of America also. Consequently, the Confederacy's constitution included the provision that only individual states would ever be capable of banning slavery. It could never be eliminated as an institution by action of their national government.

The war started when the South attacked federal Fort Sumter in the harbor of Charleston, South Carolina, on April 12, 1861. After this, President Lincoln called for 75,000 volunteers to put down the rebellion, and the South became more united than ever. On both sides, men rushed to enlist, naively fearing that the war would be over before they had a chance to fight.

The American Civil War lasted four arduous years. The war in the eastern theater, primarily

Virginia, was a stalemate for the war's duration thanks primarily to the military leadership of the South's Robert E. Lee. The battle lines went back and forth in Virginia and Maryland, with the South winning most of the battles until the latter part of the war. The war in the west, however, had a completely different outcome. Here—in Tennessee, Mississippi, and Georgia—the Northern armies, led by General Ulysses S. Grant, won most of the battles and sometimes forced the surrender of entire Southern armies that opposed them. Toward the end of the war, President Lincoln brought Grant east to oppose Lee in Virginia, and Union General William Tecumseh Sherman's army marched through the Deep South virtually unopposed.

President Abraham Lincoln, who had hated slavery all of his life, recognized during the course of the war his opportunity to strike at the heart of that institution. To do this, he realized that he would have to lead the Northern people through a significant transformation, helping them to embrace both the moral and practical benefits of eliminating slavery. On

January 1, 1863, he issued the Emancipation Proclamation, which added the elimination of slavery to the war's purposes. In speeches such as the Gettysburg Address in November 1863, Lincoln appealed to people to accept the Declaration of Independence's proposition that "*all* men are created equal." Finally, in January 1865, he pushed the acceptance of the Thirteenth Amendment, which constitutionally outlawed slavery, through a reluctant Congress. Through these efforts, he expanded the purpose of the war, as well as the minds of the Northern people. By the end of 1864, the majority of Northerners supported the elimination of slavery as a war measure to help defeat the South and/or as a morally justified action.

The American Civil War touched virtually everyone living within the boundaries of the continental United States. As will be seen, it was "fought" not only by soldiers, but also by wives, nurses, slaves, mothers, and sometimes children. Their reasons for fighting, their experiences, their hopes and fears are presented in the following pages.

Distant Drums

THE INHERENT CONFLICT between America's two foundational documents—the Declaration of Independence and the Constitution—made the Civil War inevitable. In 1776, the Founding Fathers had ideologically proclaimed in the Declaration that all men are created equal. But when they adopted the United States Constitution eleven years later, they allowed the continuation of slavery.

Most of the Founding Founders had hoped that slavery would eventually experience a peaceful demise. But by the middle of the nineteenth century, long after the Founders had died, that peaceful end remained elusive. Slavery had been instrumental in the rise of two different cultures in America, Northern and Southern. Each society feared domination by the other, and this fear evolved into mistrust. Visionaries like Robert E. Lee and William Tecumseh Sherman tried to warn America of the horrors of war, but their voices were lost in the clamor for arms.

I appear this evening as a thief and robber. I stole this head, these limbs, this body from my master and ran off with them.[2]

—Abolitionist and former slave Frederick Douglass

No, you dare not make war on cotton. No power on earth dares to make war upon it. Cotton is king![3]

—Southern Senator John Henry Hammond, regarding the antebellum South's slave-based economy

Abolitionist John Brown
"The crimes of this guilty land will never be
purged away; but with blood!"[4]

You may dispose of me very easily. I am nearly disposed of now. But this question is still to be settled, this Negro question, I mean; the end of that is not yet.[5]

> —*Abolitionist John Brown, during his trial for*
> *inciting a slave revolt*

They [persons of African descent] had for more than a century before been regarded as beings of an inferior order, and altogether unfit to associate with the white race, either in social or political relations; and so far inferior, that they had no rights which the white man was bound to respect; and that the Negro might justly and lawfully be reduced to slavery for his benefit.[6]

> —*Chief Justice of the U.S. Supreme Court Roger*
> *B. Taney, in the 1857 Dred Scott Decision*

The roaring of the approaching storm is heard from every part of the Southern states.[7]

> —*Southern slave owner and secessionist*
> *Edmund Ruffin*

In firing his gun, John Brown has merely told what time of day it is. It is high noon, thank God.[8]

> —*Abolitionist William Lloyd Garrison*

African slavery is the cornerstone of the industrial, social, and political fabric of the South; and whatever wars against it, wars against her very existence. Strike down the institution of African slavery and you reduce the South to depopulation and barbarism.[9]

> —*Southern Congressman Lawrence Keitt*

We were no more than dogs. If they caught us with a piece of paper in our pockets, they'd whip us. They was afraid we'd learn to read and write, but I never got the chance.[10]

—*A former slave woman*

This will be a great day in our history; the date of a New Revolution—quite as much needed as the old one. Even now as I write they are leading old John Brown to execution in Virginia for attempting to rescue slaves! This is sowing the wind to reap the whirlwind, which will come soon![11]

—*Henry Wadsworth Longfellow*

I think we must get rid of slavery, or we must get rid of freedom.[12]

—*Ralph Waldo Emerson*

The great difference…is the institution of slavery. This alone sets apart the Southern States as a peculiar people, with whom independence, as to their internal policy, is the condition of their existence. They must rule themselves or perish.[13]

> —*Southern secessionist Robert Barnwell Rhett Sr.*

The leading Northern politicians…do not believe that there is either courage or strength enough in the South to resist these efforts… Never has there been such an opportunity for secession.[14]

> —*Southern slave owner and secessionist*
> *Edmund Ruffin*

[Slavery is] the Mightiest Engine in the world for the civilization, education, and refinement of mankind.[15]

—Confederate General John Brown Gordon

We have here only one life to live, and once to die; and if we lose our lives it will perhaps do more for the cause than our lives would be worth in any other way.[16]

—Abolitionist John Brown

If the slaves of the South were mine, I would surrender them all without a struggle to avert the war.[17]

—Confederate General Robert E. Lee

We shall fire the Southern heart—instruct the Southern mind—give courage to each other, and at the proper moment, by one organized, concerted action, we can precipitate the cotton states into a revolution.[18]

—*Southern slave owner and secessionist William Lowndes Yancey*

I believe that to interfere, as I have done, in the behalf of God's despised poor is not wrong but right. Now, if it is deemed necessary that I should forfeit my life for the furtherance of the ends of justice, and mingle my blood further with the blood of my children and with the blood of millions in this slave country whose rights are disregarded by wicked, cruel, and unjust enactments, I say, let it be done.[19]

—*Abolitionist John Brown, shortly before being hanged for inciting a slave revolt*

He is not Old Brown any longer; he is an angel of light.[20]

> —*Henry David Thoreau, speaking of the martyred John Brown*

They do not know what they say. If it comes to a conflict of arms, the war will last at least four years. Northern politicians do not appreciate the determination and pluck of the South, and Southern politicians do not appreciate the numbers, resources, and patient perseverance of the North. Both sides forget that we are all Americans. I foresee that the country will have to pass through a terrible ordeal, a necessary expiation, perhaps, for our national sins.[21]

> —*Confederate General Robert E. Lee*

You, you the people of the South, believe there can be such a thing as peaceable secession. You don't know what you are doing… This country will be drenched in blood. God only knows how it will end.[22]

—*Union General William Tecumseh Sherman*

We seem to be drifting to destruction before our eyes, in utter helplessness.[23]

—*Northern Congressman Caleb Cushing*

We are going to destruction as fast as we can.[24]

—*Confederate Vice President Alexander Hamilton Stephens*

Some of you laugh to scorn the idea of blood-
shed as the result of secession, and jocularly
propose to drink all the blood that will ever
flow in consequence of it. But let me tell you
what is coming on the heels of secession… You
may, after the sacrifice of countless millions of
treasure and of hundreds of thousands of pre-
cious lives, as a bare possibility, win Southern
independence, if God be not against you, but
I doubt it. I tell you that, while I believe with
you in the doctrine of state rights, the North
is determined to preserve this Union. They are
not a fiery, impulsive people as you are, for they
live in colder climates. But when they begin to
move in a given direction, where great interests
are involved, such as the present issue before the
country, they move with the steady momentum
and perseverance of a mighty avalanche; and
what I fear is, they will overwhelm the South
with ignoble defeat.[25]

> —*Texas Governor Sam Houston, talking to*
> *fellow Southerners who wanted secession*

The people of the South and those of the North are essentially two races of men, with habits of thought and action very unlike.[26]

—Southern secessionist Albert Pike

I think it is to be a long war—very long— much longer than any politician thinks.[27]

—Union General William Tecumseh Sherman

Better lose a million men in battle than allow the government to be overthrown. The war will soon assume the shape of Slavery and Freedom. The world will so understand it, and I believe the final outcome will redound to the good of humanity.[28]

—Future U.S. president James A. Garfield

Free society! We sicken at the name. What is it [the North] but a conglomeration of greasy mechanics, filthy operatives, small-fisted farmers, and moonstruck theorists?… The prevailing class one meets with is that of mechanics struggling to be genteel, and small farmers that do their own drudgery, and yet are hardly fit for association with a Southern gentleman's body servant.[29]

> —*A Georgia newspaper, talking about the Northern people*

Slavery cannot share a government with democracy.[30]

> —*Southern secessionist Leonidas W. Spratt*

Secession asserts the principle that the minority have the right to force the majority. There can be no government where such a principle is recognized.[31]

—*Southern Judge Garnett Andrews*

I will never give rest to my eyes nor slumber to my eyelids until [the Union] is shattered into pieces.[32]

—*Southern secessionist Nathaniel Beverley Tucker*

No power can prevent [secession]. Our destiny seems to be fixed.[33]

—*Confederate Vice President Alexander Hamilton Stephens*

The time for war has not yet come, but it will come, and that soon; and when it does come, my advice is to draw the sword and throw away the scabbard.[34]

—*Confederate General Stonewall Jackson*

All they want is to get you to fight for their infernal Negroes, and after you do their fightin', you may kiss their hin' parts for all they care.[35]

—*Southern farmer from Winston County, Alabama, talking about the slave owners*

We will fight you to the death! Better to die a thousand deaths than to submit to live under you.[36]

—*Confederate General John Bell Hood*

In thinking of America, I sometimes find myself admiring her bright blue sky, her grand old woods, her fertile fields, her beautiful rivers, her mighty lakes and star-crowned mountains. But my rapture is soon checked when I remember that all is cursed with the infernal spirit of slave holding and wrong; When I remember that with the waters of her noblest rivers, the tears of my brethren are borne to the ocean, disregarded and forgotten; That her most fertile fields drink daily of the warm blood of my outraged sisters, I am filled with unutterable loathing.[37]

> —Abolitionist and former slave
> Frederick Douglass

This step, secession, once taken, can never be recalled… We and our posterity shall see our lovely South desolated by the demon of war.[38]

> —Confederate Vice President Alexander
> Hamilton Stephens

I am aware that many object to the severity of my language, but is there not cause for severity? I will be as harsh as truth, and as uncompromising as justice. On this subject I do not wish to think, or speak, or write, with moderation... I am in earnest—I will not equivocate—I will not excuse—I will not retreat a single inch—and I will be heard.[39]

> —*Abolitionist William Lloyd Garrison, in his newspaper,* The Liberator

☆☆☆

I am decided; my course is fixed; my path is blazed. The Union and the Constitution shall be preserved and the laws enforced at every and at all hazards.[40]

> —*President Abraham Lincoln*

The time for compromise has now passed. The South is determined to maintain her position, and make all who oppose her smell Southern powder and feel Southern steel![41]

—*Confederate President Jefferson Davis*

The firing on that fort will inaugurate a civil war greater than any the world has yet seen… At this time it is suicide, murder, and will lose us every friend at the North… You will wantonly strike a hornet's nest… It is unnecessary; it puts us in the wrong; it is fatal.[42]

—*Confederate Secretary of State Robert Toombs, warning against the South's impending attack on the Union's Fort Sumter*

2

Call to Arms

IN APRIL OF 1861, eleven Southern states had either seceded or were about to secede from the Union. In his First Inaugural Address, Abraham Lincoln had tried to assure his "dissatisfied fellow countrymen" that war was not necessary—that the U.S. government would not assail them— unless the South was itself "the aggressor." But as each Southern state joined the Confederacy, the people's excitement in becoming an independent nation increased, and emotions in the South rose to a feverish pitch. It was with incredible naivety that men on both sides rushed off to join in a war they thought would be easily won. The federal government's Fort Sumter, located in the middle of Charleston Harbor, became the war's flash point when Southern soldiers attacked it on the morning of April 12, 1861.

★★★

At half-past four, the heavy booming of a cannon. I sprang out of bed. And on my knees—prostrate—I prayed as I never prayed before.[43]

> —*Southern diarist Mary Boykin Chesnut, upon hearing the guns beginning the war at Fort Sumter*

Our Southern brethren have done grievously wrong, they have rebelled and have attacked their father's house and their loyal brothers. They must be punished and brought back, but this necessity breaks my heart.[44]

> —*Union Major Robert Anderson, after being forced to surrender Fort Sumter*

So Civil War is inaugurated at last. God defend the right.[45]

> —*Northern diarist George Templeton Strong*

*Abolitionist and former
slave Frederick Douglass*
*"What a change now greets us! The Government
is aroused, the dead North is alive, and its divided
people united… The cry now is for war, vigorous
war, war to the bitter end, and war till the traitors are effectually and permanently put down."*[46]

South Carolina is too small for a republic and too large for an insane asylum.[47]

> —*Southern Judge James L. Petigru, upon hearing that South Carolina had seceded from the Union*

We looked forward to the time when we could give the Yankees a taste of our steel, and we were confident that when the time came we would be victorious.[48]

> —*Confederate soldier Robert S. Hudgins*

We seceded to rid ourselves of the rule of the majority.[49]

> —*Confederate President Jefferson Davis*

You have made the greatest mistake of your life, but I feared it would be so.[50]

> —Union General Winfield Scott, to Confederate
> General Robert E. Lee, who declined Scott's offer
> to take command of the Union armies

The die was cast; war was declared…every person, almost, was eager for the war, and we were all afraid it would be over and we not be in the fight.[51]

> —Confederate soldier Sam Watkins

To fight against slaveholders, without fighting against slavery, is but a halfhearted business… Fire must be met with water… War for the destruction of liberty must be met with war for the destruction of slavery.[52]

> —Abolitionist and former slave
> Frederick Douglass

I know how strongly American Civilization now leans on the triumph of the Government, and how great a debt we owe to those who went before us through the blood and sufferings of the Revolution. And I am willing—perfectly will-ing—to lay down all my joys in this life, to help maintain this Government, and to pay that debt.[53]

—*Union soldier Sullivan Ballou*

☆☆☆

The young men carry dress suits with them. Every soldier, nearly, has a servant with him, and a whole lot of spoons and forks, so as to live comfortably and elegantly in camp, and finally to make a splurge in Washington when they shall arrive there, which they expect will be very soon.[54]

—*A Southern woman in Rome, Georgia*

There are only two sides to the question. Every man must be for the United States or against it. There can be no neutrals in this war, only patriots—or traitors![55]

—*Northern Senator Stephen A. Douglas*

Of the civil war I say only this… It is Slavery against Freedom; the North wind against the Southern pestilence. I saw lately, at a jeweler's, a slave's collar of iron, with an iron tongue as large as a spoon, to go into the mouth. Every drop of blood in me quivered! The world forgets what slavery really is![56]

—*Henry Wadsworth Longfellow*

This is a death struggle and will be terrible.[57]

—*Union General William Tecumseh Sherman*

I will receive 200 able-bodied men if they will present themselves at my headquarters by the first of June with good horse and gun. I wish none but those who desire to be actively engaged. My headquarters for the present is at Corinth, Miss. Come on, boys, if you want a heap of fun and to kill some Yankees.[58]

—*Confederate General Nathan Bedford Forrest*

Once let the black man get upon his person the brass letters, U.S.; let him get an eagle on his button, and a musket on his shoulder and bullets in his pocket, and there is no power on earth which can deny that he has earned the right to citizenship.[59]

—*Abolitionist and former slave*
Frederick Douglass

While our soldiers fight, I can stand and feed
and nurse them. My place is anywhere between
the bullet and the battlefield.[60]
> —*Union nurse Clara Barton*

I express it as my conviction before God that
it is the duty of every American citizen to rally
round the flag of his country.[61]
> —*Northern Senator Stephen A. Douglas*

I long to be a man, but as I can't fight, I will
content myself with working for those who can.[62]
> —*Northern author and nurse Louisa May Alcott*

Our new Government is founded upon…
its cornerstone rests, upon the great truth that
the Negro is not equal to the white man; that
slavery, subordination to the superior race, is
his natural and moral condition. This, our new
Government, is the first, in the history of the
world, based upon this great physical, philo-
sophical, and moral truth. This truth has been
slow in the process of its development, like all
other truths in the various departments of sci-
ence. It is so even amongst us. Many who hear
me, perhaps, can recollect well that this truth
was not generally admitted, even within their
day. The errors of the past generation still clung
to many as late as twenty years ago. Those at
the North, who still cling to these errors, with
a zeal above knowledge, we justly denominate
fanatics. All fanaticism springs from an aberra-
tion of the mind, from a defect in reasoning. It
is a species of insanity. One of the most striking
characteristics of insanity, in many instances,
is forming correct conclusions from fancied

or erroneous premises; so with the antislavery
fanatics: their conclusions are right if their
premises are. They assume that the Negro is
equal, and hence conclude that he is entitled to
equal privileges and rights with the white man.[63]
—*Confederate Vice President Alexander
Hamilton Stephens*

These new [soldiers] are running in… They
fear the war will be over before they get a sight
of the fun. Every man from every little country
precinct wants a place in the picture.[64]
—*Southern diarist Mary Boykin Chesnut*

We feel that our cause is just and holy.[65]
—*Confederate President Jefferson Davis*

We are battling for our rights and homes.
Ours is a just war, a holy cause. The invader
must meet the fate he deserves and we must
meet him as becomes us, as becomes men.[66]
—*Confederate Major John Pelham*

I want to fight until we win the cause so many
have died for. I don't believe in Secession, but I
do in Liberty. I want the South to conquer, dic-
tate its own terms, and go back to the Union,
for I believe that, apart, inevitable ruin awaits
both. It is a rope of sand, this Confederacy,
founded on the doctrine of Secession, and will
not last many years—not five.[67]
—*Southern diarist Sarah Morgan Dawson*

The army of the South will be composed of
the best material that ever yet made up an army;
while that of Lincoln will be gathered from
the sewers of the cities—the degraded, beastly
outscoring of all the quarters of the world, who
will serve for pay and will run away as soon as
they can when danger threatens.[68]

> —The Raleigh *[North Carolina]* Banner

☆☆☆

Mine eyes have seen the glory of the coming
of the Lord:
He is trampling out the vintage where the
grapes of wrath are stored;
He hath loosed the fateful lightning of His terrible swift sword:
His truth is marching on.[69]

> —*Abolitionist Julia Ward Howe, from the song*
> *"Battle Hymn of the Republic"*

It is not alone a fight between the North and the South; it is a fight between freedom and slavery; between God and the devil; between heaven and hell.[70]

> —Republican Congressman George
> Washington Julian

We are a band of brothers, and natives to the soil,
Fighting for the property we gained by honest toil;
And when our rights were threatened, the cry rose near and far:
Hurrah for the bonnie Blue Flag that bears the single star![71]

> —Southern songwriter Harry McCarthy, from
> the song "Bonnie Blue Flag"

A law was made by the Confederate States Congress about this time allowing every person who owned twenty Negroes to go home. It gave us the blues; we wanted twenty Negroes. Negro property suddenly became very valuable, and there was raised the howl of "rich man's war, poor man's fight."[72]

— *Confederate soldier Sam Watkins*

3

A Resolve to Win

At the Civil War's inception, both sides underestimated the other's resolve to win. Southerners believed that their soldiers, who were typically more familiar with guns and horses than their Northern counterparts, would quickly prove the Yankees to be cowardly and unworthy opponents. Northerners dismissed Southern bravado and were confident that their well-equipped armies would quickly overwhelm their enemies. Soldiers of both sides feared that the war would be over in a matter of weeks and that they would not get an opportunity to fight.

They were both wrong. The North underestimated the Southern people's resolve to persevere in spite of fewer resources, as well as their motivational advantage of "defending their homes." The South underestimated the Northern people's resolve to keep fighting for the Union in spite of suffering tremendous casualties on the battlefields.

We must do more than defeat their armies. We must destroy them.[73]
>   —*Confederate General Stonewall Jackson*

Look, men! There stands Jackson like a stone wall. Rally behind the Virginians![74]
>   —*Confederate General Barnard Elliott Bee Jr.,*
>   *pointing out General Stonewall Jackson at the*
>   *Battle of First Manassas*

Union Army nurse Clara Barton
"If I cannot be a soldier, I'll help soldiers."[75]

I have served my country under the flag of the Union for more than fifty years, and as long as God permits me to live, I will defend that flag with my sword; even if my own native State assails it.[76]

> —*Union General and Virginian Winfield Scott, to representatives of the Confederacy offering him command*

I'm fighting because you are down here.[77]

> —*A Confederate soldier, when asked why he fought*

I would fight them if they were a million. The more men they crowd in there, the worse we can make it for them.[78]

> —*Confederate General Albert Sidney Johnston, prior to Shiloh*

O if I was only a man! Then I would don the breeches, and slay them with a will! If some Southern women were in the ranks, they would set the men an example they would not blush to follow![79]

—*Southern diarist Sarah Morgan Dawson*

Retreat? No. I propose to attack at daylight and whip them.[80]

>—*Union General Ulysses S. Grant, to his subordinates, after nearly being defeated in the first day's battle at Shiloh*

Now those Yankees were whipped, fairly whipped, and according to all the rules of war they ought to have retreated. But they didn't.[81]

>—*Confederate soldier Sam Watkins, after the first day of the Battle of Shiloh*

What I want, and what the people want, is generals who will fight battles and win victories. Grant has done this, and I propose to stand by him.[82]

—*President Abraham Lincoln, defending Ulysses S. Grant after Shiloh*

General Grant habitually wears an expression as if he had determined to drive his head through a brick wall and was about to do it.[83]

—*Union Colonel Theodore Lyman III*

You may hiss as much as you please, but women will get their rights anyway. You can't stop us, neither.[84]

—*Former slave Sojourner Truth to hecklers in a crowd*

There is nothing on this green earth half so grand as the sight of soldiers moving into action. A cavalry charge is superb; artillery dashing on the field carries you away; while the deadly infantry moving into the jaws of death causes you to hold your breath in admiration.[85]

—*Confederate soldier William H. Andrews*

I can't spare this man. He fights.[86]

—*President Abraham Lincoln, answering a critic of Ulysses S. Grant*

His zeal in the cause of freedom was infinitely superior to mine. Mine was as the taper light; his was as the burning sun. I could live for the slave; John Brown could die for him.[87]

—*Abolitionist and former slave Frederick Douglass*

Up to the battle of Shiloh, I, as well as thousands of other citizens, believed that the rebellion against the Government would collapse suddenly and soon, if a decisive victory could be gained over any of its armies…[but after] I gave up all idea of saving the Union except by complete conquest.[88]

—*Union General Ulysses S. Grant*

Excepting John Brown, of sacred memory, I know of no one who has willingly encountered more perils and hardships to serve our enslaved people than you have. Much that you have done would seem improbable to those who do not know you as I know you.[89]

—*Abolitionist and former slave Frederick*
Douglass, talking to Harriet Tubman

Sarah, my love for you is deathless, it seems to
bind me with mighty cables that nothing but
Omnipotence could break; and yet my love of
Country comes over me like a strong wind and
bears me unresistibly on with all these chains
to the battlefield… I have, I know, but few
and small claims upon Divine Providence, but
something whispers to me—perhaps it is the
wafted prayer of my little Edgar, that I shall
return to my loved ones unharmed. If I do not,
my dear Sarah, never forget how much I love
you, and when my last breath escapes me on the
battlefield, it will whisper your name.[90]

> —*Union soldier Sullivan Ballou, in a letter to*
> *his wife*

If we oppose force to force we cannot win, for
their resources are greater than ours. We must
substitute esprit for numbers.[91]

> —*Confederate General J. E. B. Stuart*

It is said that Lincoln has called for 500,000 more men. Numbers have now no terror for the Southern people. They are willing to wage the war against quadruple their number.[92]

—*Confederate War Clerk John B. Jones*

I have never in my life taken a command into battle and had the slightest desire to come out alive unless I won.[93]

—*Union General Philip H. Sheridan*

A series of braver, more desperate charges than those hurled against the troops in the sunken road was never known, and the piles and cross-piles of dead marked a field such as I never saw before or since.[94]

—*Confederate General James Longstreet,*
speaking of the Union attack at Fredericksburg

The first thing I met was a regiment of the vilest odors that ever assaulted the human nose, and took it by storm…[then] there they were, "our brave boys," as the papers justly called them, for cowards could hardly have been so riddled with shot and shell, so torn and shattered, nor have borne suffering for which we have no name, with an uncomplaining fortitude, which made one glad to cherish each other as a brother.[95]

—*Union nurse Louisa May Alcott, describing the wounded from Fredericksburg*

The enemy is advancing in strong force, I will fight him inch by inch, and if driven into the town I will barricade the streets and hold him back as long as possible.[96]

—*Union General John Fulton Reynolds*

I had crossed the line of which I had so long been dreaming. I was free; but there was no one to welcome me to the land of freedom, I was a stranger in a strange land, and my home after all was down in the old cabin quarter, with the old folks, and my brothers and sisters. But to this solemn resolution I came; I was free, and they should be free also; I would make a home for them in the North, and the Lord helping me, I would bring them all there.[97]

—*Former slave and abolitionist*
Harriet Tubman

If you don't have my army supplied, and keep it supplied, we'll eat your mules up, sir.[98]

—*Union General William Tecumseh Sherman,*
talking to a Union quartermaster

There will be some black men who can remember that, with silent tongue, and clenched teeth, and a steady eye, and well-poised bayonet, they have helped mankind on to this great consummation; while, I fear, there will be some white ones, unable to forget that, with malignant heart, and deceitful speech, they have strove to hinder it.[99]

—*President Abraham Lincoln*

Grief and anxiety kill nearly as many women as men die on the battlefield.[100]

—*Southern diarist Mary Boykin Chesnut*

Let danger never turn you aside from the pursuit of honor or the service of your country.[101]

—*Confederate General Robert E. Lee*

The sight of several stretchers, each with its leg-less, armless, or desperately wounded occupant, entering my ward, admonished me that I was there to work, not to wonder or weep; so I corked up my feelings, and returned to the path of duty, which was "rather a hard road to travel," just then.[102]

> —*Union nurse Louisa May Alcott*

If it must be, let it come, and when there is no longer a soldier's arm to raise the Stars and Stripes above our Capitol, may God give me strength to mine.[103]

> —*Union nurse Clara Barton*

Gentlemen, I know of no better place to die than right here.[104]

> —*Union General George Henry Thomas, at a*
> *council of war*

Indeed in this war more truly than in any other the spirit of lovely woman points the dart, hurls the javelin, ignites the mine, pulls the trigger, draws the lanyard and gives a fiercer truer temper to the blade in far more literal sense than the mere muscular aggressions of man.[105]

—*Confederate General J. E. B. Stuart*

We are fighting for independence, and that, or extermination, we will have… We will govern ourselves…if we have to see every Southern plantation sacked, and every Southern city in flames.[106]

—*Confederate President Jefferson Davis*

We lost color bearer after color bearer, I picked up the colors three times myself. The flagstaff was shot off and the flag perforated in 19 places by Rebel bullets.[107]

> —*Union Lieutenant Daniel R. Coders,*
> *speaking of a Union charge at Gettysburg*

This year has brought about many changes that at the beginning were or would have been thought impossible. The close of the year finds me a soldier for the cause of my race. May God bless the cause, and enable me in the coming year to forward it on.[108]

> —*Union soldier and free black*
> *Christopher A. Fleetwood*

4

Character

WAR, MORE THAN anything, brings out the true character of a people. Hatred of the enemy generally grows as the killing and suffering increase, but the American Civil War was unique in that many soldiers had friends and relatives on their adversary's side. Opposing generals on the battlefield openly admired the courage displayed by their enemies in an attack. Soldiers of rival armies sometimes called informal truces, traded tobacco for coffee, and bantered with their foes.

The people's ability to persevere in this "brother's war" was a result of many character traits—their faith in God, their belief in the righteousness of their cause, and sometimes their sense of humor. Hatred of the enemy was not uncommon in the Civil War, but underlying it was the widespread belief that their antagonists were simply well-meaning, misguided fellow Americans.

It is my constant anxiety and prayer that I and this nation should be on the Lord's side.[109]

—*President Abraham Lincoln*

My religious belief teaches me to feel as safe in battle as in bed. God has fixed the time for my death. I do not concern myself about that but to be always ready, no matter when it may overtake me. That is the way all men should live, and then all would be equally brave.[110]

—*Confederate General Stonewall Jackson*

Confederate General
Thomas J. (Stonewall) Jackson
"As a Christian I wouldn't like to see war, but as a soldier, sir, I would like to see war."[111]

Our opponents finally began lowering their guns, which we took and threw behind us. Then at once we became friends and began a frenzied trading of tobacco for coffee.[112]

—*Confederate soldier James M. Weiser*

The rifle and musket balls have been whizzing round our heads so much that we don't notice them as much as we would a bumble bee at home.[113]

—*Union Lieutenant Thomas McClure*

So many men were daily struck in the camp and trenches that men became utterly reckless, passing about where balls were striking as though it was their normal life and making a joke of a narrow escape or a noisy, whistling ball.[114]

—*Union General David S. Stanley*

I don't know but that God has created some one man great enough to comprehend the whole of this stupendous crisis and transaction from beginning to end, and endowed him with sufficient wisdom to manage and direct it. I confess I do not fully understand, and foresee it all. But I am placed here where I am obliged to the best of my poor ability to deal with it.[115]

> —*President Abraham Lincoln*

You appear much concerned at my attacking on Sunday. I was greatly concerned, too; but...so far as I can see, my course was a wise one...though very distasteful to my feelings; and I hope and pray to our Heavenly Father that I may never again be circumstanced as on that day.[116]

> —*Confederate General Stonewall Jackson, in a letter to his wife*

Dear Brother, I was astonished to hear from the prisoners that you was colour bearer of the Regmt that assalted the Battrey at this point the other day. When I first heard it I looked over the field for you where I met one of the wounded of your Regt and he told me that he believed you was safe. I was in the Brest work during the whole engagement doing my Best to Beat you but I hope that you and I will never again meet face to face Bitter enemies in the Battle field. But if such should be the case You have but to discharge your deauty to Your caus for I can assure you I will strive to discharge my deauty to my country & my cause.[117]

> —*Confederate soldier James Campbell, writing to his brother Alexander, whom he had fought against at the Battle of Secessionville, South Carolina*

I can't die but once.[118]

> —*Former slave and abolitionist Harriet Tubman*

War ennobles the age. We do not often have a moment of grandeur in these hurried, slipshod lives, but the behavior of the young men has taught us much. We will not again disparage America, now that we have seen what men it will bear.[119]

—*Ralph Waldo Emerson*

☆☆☆

Lord! What a scramble there'll be for arms and legs, when we old boys come out of our graves, on Judgment Day: wonder if we shall get our own again? If we do, my leg will have to tramp from Fredericksburg, my arm from here, I suppose, and meet my body, wherever it may be.[120]

—*A Union sergeant, to nurse Louisa May Alcott*

The first thing in the morning is drill, then drill, then drill again. Then drill, drill, a little more drill. Then drill, and lastly drill. Between drills, we drill and sometimes stop to eat a little and have a roll call.[121]

—*Union soldier Oliver Willcox Norton*

He [Ulysses S. Grant] had somehow, with all his modesty, the rare faculty of controlling his superiors as well as his subordinates. He outfaced [Secretary of War] Stanton, captivated the President, and even compelled acquiescence or silence from that dread source of paralyzing power, the Congressional Committee on the Conduct of the War.[122]

—*Union General Joshua Lawrence
Chamberlain*

I have fought against the people of the North because I believed they were seeking to wrest from the South dearest rights. But I have never cherished toward them bitter or vindictive feelings, and have never seen the day when I did not pray for them.[123]

—*Confederate General Robert E. Lee*

I must say, and I am proud to say, that I never was treated by anyone with more kindness and cordiality than was shown me by the great and good man, Abraham Lincoln, by the grace of God president of the United States.[124]

—*Former slave Sojourner Truth*

Will the slave fight? If any man asks you, tell him no. But if anyone asks you will a Negro fight, tell him yes![125]

—*Abolitionist Wendell Phillips*

Now it seems strange to me that we do not receive the same pay and rations as the white soldiers. Do we not fill the same ranks? Do we not cover the same space of ground? Do we not take up the same length of ground in a grave-yard that others do? The ball does not miss the black man and strike the white, nor the white and strike the black.[126]

—*Union soldier Edward L. Washington*

I was never more quickly or more completely put at ease in the presence of a great man, than in that of Abraham Lincoln… I at once felt myself in the presence of an honest man—one whom I could love, honor, and trust without reserve or doubt.[127]

—*Abolitionist and former slave*
Frederick Douglass

I had a right to my own political opinions... I am a Southern woman, born with revolutionary blood in my veins... Freedom of speech and of thought were my birthright, guaranteed by our charter of liberty, the Constitution of the United States, and signed and sealed by the blood of our fathers.[128]

—*Southern spy Rose O'Neal Greenhow*

I don't know how long it has been since my ear has been free from the roll of a drum. It is the music I sleep by, and I love it... I shall remain here while anyone remains, and do whatever comes to my hand. I may be compelled to face danger, but never fear it, and while our soldiers can stand and fight, I can stand and feed and nurse them.[129]

—*Union nurse Clara Barton*

In the very responsible position in which I
happen to be placed, being an humble instrument in the hands of our Heavenly Father, as I
am and as we all are, to work out his great purposes, I have desired that all my works and acts
may be according to his will, and that it might
be so, I have sought his aid.[130]

            —*President Abraham Lincoln*

For a mile up and down the open fields before
us the splendid lines of the veterans of the
Army of Northern Virginia swept down upon
us. Their bearing was magnificent. They came
forward with a rush, and how our men did yell,
"Come on, Johnny, come on!"[131]

            —*Union General Rufus R. Dawes,*
            of the Iron Brigade

If this war has developed some of the most brutal, bestial, and devilish qualities lurking in the human race, it has also shown how much of the angel there is in the best men and women.[132]

> —*Union nurse and writer Mary Ashton*
> *Rice Livermore*

The brave Union commander, superbly mounted, placed himself in front, while his band cheered them with martial music. I thought, "What a pity to spoil with bullets such a scene of martial beauty."[133]

> —*Confederate General John Brown Gordon*

Sherman will never go to Hell. He'll outflank the Devil and make heaven in spite of the guards.[134]

> —*A Confederate soldier*

I did not like to stand and be shot at without shooting back.[135]

>—Twelve-year-old Union drummer boy John Clem, who threw down his drum and picked up a gun in the Battle of Chickamauga

Sherman probably carries a spare tunnel, anyway.[136]

>—An unimpressed Confederate soldier, upon hearing that Confederate raiders had collapsed a tunnel along Sherman's supply line

Since I am here I have learned and seen more of what the horrors of Slavery was than I ever knew before and I am glad indeed that the signs of the time show towards closing out the accused institution.[137]

>—Union soldier Marcus M. Spiegel

I hate newspapermen. They come into camp and pick up their camp rumors and print them as facts. I regard them as spies, which, in truth, they are. If I killed them all there would be news from Hell before breakfast.[138]

—*Union General William Tecumseh Sherman*

There are blackberries in the fields so our boys and the Yanks made a bargain not to fire at each other, and went out in the field, leaving one man on each post with the arms, and gathered berries together and talked over the fight, and traded tobacco and coffee and newspapers as peacefully and kindly as if they had not been engaged for…seven days in butchering one another.[139]

—*A Confederate soldier*

So now I am minus a leg! But never mind, dear parents. I suffer but little pain, and will [be] home in a few weeks, I think.[140]

—*Union soldier William V. H. Cortelyou*

I can only say that I am nothing but a poor sinner, trusting in Christ alone for salvation.[141]

—*Confederate General Robert E. Lee*

He who does not see the hand of God in this is blind, sir, blind![142]

—*Confederate General Stonewall Jackson, after a victory*

5

War Is Hell

THE CIVIL WAR claimed over 620,000 lives, which is nearly as many as all the nation's other wars combined. Union General William Tecumseh Sherman—a friend of the South in times of peace, but its worst enemy during the war—became the first modern advocate of "total war." When civilians of the South clamored for the gentle treatment that Confederate General Lee and Union General McClellan had provided civilians in the east, Sherman refused. He believed that the North would never defeat the Southern people without causing them to "sicken" of war. His infamous sixty-mile-wide swath of destruction across the state of Georgia was made for the explicit purpose of breaking the South's will to fight. By war's end, both Northerners and Southerners, and generals like

William Tecumseh Sherman, had grown to hate
the terrible oppressions of war.

Damn the torpedoes! Full speed ahead![143]
                    —*Union Admiral David Glasgow Farragut*

Free every slave, slay every traitor, burn every
Rebel mansion—if these things be necessary to
preserve this temple of freedom to the world
and to our posterity. Unless we do this, we
cannot conquer them.[144]
                    —*Northern Congressman Thaddeus Stevens*

We may be annihilated, but we cannot
be conquered.[145]
                    —*Confederate General Albert Sidney Johnston*

*Union General William
Tecumseh Sherman*
"War is Hell."[146]

We cannot change the hearts of those people of the South, but we can make war so terrible, make them so sick of war that generations would pass away before they would again appeal to it.[147]

—*Union General William Tecumseh Sherman*

I am tired of the battlefield, with its mangled corpses and poor wounded. Victory has no charms for me when purchased at such a cost.[148]

—*Union General George B. McClellan*

There was, on the part of the men, great hysterical excitement, eagerness to go forward, and a reckless disregard of life, of everything but victory.[149]

—*Union General Rufus R. Dawes*

Where men fell and left a vacant place other men stepped into their places and although death stared us in the face there was not a man who faltered.[150]

—*Union soldier Josiah F. Murphey*

I did not think any more of seeing a man shot down by my side than you would of seeing a dumb beast killed. Strange as it may seem to you, but the more men I saw killed the more reckless I became.[151]

—*Union soldier Franklin Bailey, in a letter to his parents*

The scenes on this field would have cured anybody of war.[152]

—*Union General William Tecumseh Sherman, regarding Shiloh*

I hope that I may never see such a sight again.
The dead were thicker here than I had seen
them anywhere else.[153]

> —*Union soldier Tully McCrea, at*
> *the Battle of Antietam*

Shiloh was the severest battle fought at the
West during the war, and but few in the East
equaled it for hard, determined fighting. I saw
an open field, in our possession on the second
day, over which the Confederates had made
repeated charges the day before, so covered with
dead that it would have been possible to walk
across the clearing, in any direction, stepping
on dead bodies, without a foot touching
the ground.[154]

> —*Union General Ulysses S. Grant*

Those of us who were yet living got back to
the edge of the cornfield, and opened such a
fire, that, though the enemy charged five times
to gain possession of the flag, they were driven
back each time with terrible slaughter.[155]

—*Union soldier Charles B. Tanner*

As I witnessed one line swept away by one
fearful blast from Kershaw's men behind the
stone wall, I forgot they were enemies and only
remembered that they were men, and it is hard
to see in cold blood brave men die.[156]

—*Confederate soldier Alexander Hunter, at
Fredericksburg*

I would charge hell itself for that old man![157]

—*Confederate soldier Robert Campbell, talking
about General Robert E. Lee*

All night we made compresses and slings—and
bound up and wet wounds, when we could get
water, fed what we could, travelled miles in that
dark over these poor helpless wretches, in terror
lest some one's candle fall into the hay and
consume them all.[158]

> —*Union nurse Clara Barton, talking about*
> *nursing three thousand wounded soldiers that*
> *were lying in a field*

The sight of these poor, stricken men as
they helped one another, as they bound one
another's wounds, as they painfully hobbled
to and fro for water, was a most pathetic one.
They lined the roadside for half a mile, a double
hedgerow of suffering and death, as men were
dying in the fence corners every few minutes.[159]

> —*Union soldier Frank Wilkeson,*
> *at the Battle of the Wilderness*

Over five thousand dead and wounded men were on the ground in every attitude of distress. A third of them were dead or dying, but enough were alive and moving to give to the field a singular crawling effect.[160]

—*Union General William Woods Averell*

☆☆☆

I saw him sitting there gently reclined against the tree, essentially old, this boy of scarcely sixteen summers. His cap had fallen to the ground on one side, his hand resting on his knee. It clasped a little testament opened at some familiar place. He wore the gray. He was my enemy, this boy. He was dead—the boy, my enemy—but I shall see him forever.[161]

—*Union General Joshua Lawrence Chamberlain*

The balls were whizzing so thick that it looked like a man could hold out a hat and catch it full.[162]

—*A Confederate soldier at Gettysburg*

I never had a clear conception of the horrors of war until that night and the morning. Ongoing round on that battlefield with a candle searching for my friends I could hear on all sides the dreadful groans of the wounded and their heart piercing cries for water and assistance. Friends and foes all together.[163]

—*Confederate soldier Andrew Nelson Erskine*

I never saw troops behave more magnificently than Pickett's division of Virginians did today in that grand charge upon the enemy.[164]

—*Confederate General Robert E. Lee,*
at Gettysburg

Atlanta is ours, and fairly won.[165]

   —*Union General William Tecumseh Sherman*

☆☆☆

I have just heard one of my brothers was killed in the war. Since he chose to be our deadly enemy, I see no reason why I should bitterly mourn his death. Why should I sympathize with the Rebels? They would hang my husband tomorrow if it was in their power.[166]

   —*Mary Todd Lincoln*

☆☆☆

Darkest of all Decembers ever has my life known, sitting here by the embers, stunned, helpless, alone.[167]

   —*Southern diarist Mary Boykin Chesnut, after Sherman took Atlanta*

It is well that war is so terrible—we should grow too fond of it.[168]

—*Confederate General Robert E. Lee*

I have amputated limbs until it almost makes my heart ache to see a poor fellow coming in the Ambulance to the Hospital... The horror of this war can never be half told.[169]

—*Union surgeon Claiborne Walton*

You have no idea of the horrible noise the shells make—when one passes over your head with its scream as if fifty locomotive whistles were blowing at once, no man can help dodging.[170]

—*Union surgeon Edwin Hutchinson, in a letter to his mother*

The power they are bringing to bear against our country is tremendous. Its weight may be irresistible—I dare not think of that, however.[171]
—*Southern diarist Mary Boykin Chesnut*

War is cruelty and you cannot refine it.[172]
—*Union General William Tecumseh Sherman*

When I say that they were hungry, I convey no impression of the gaunt starvation that looked from their cavernous eyes…that they could march or fight at all seemed incredible.[173]
—*Southern woman Mary Bedinger Mitchell, talking about Confederate soldiers in Virginia*

No description of what we have endured or
what we have seen could give the slightest idea
of the horrible truth.[174]

> —*Confederate Lieutenant Colonel*
> *David R. E. Winn*

War means fighting. And fighting means
killing.[175]

> —*Confederate General Nathan Bedford Forrest*

I'm ashamed of you, dodging that way. They
couldn't hit an elephant at this distance.[176]

> —*Union General John Sedgwick,*
> *just moments before being killed by a*
> *Confederate sniper at Spotsylvania*

The peculiarity of the rebel yell is worthy
of mention, but none of the old soldiers who
heard it once will ever forget it. Instead of the
deep-chested manly cheer of the Union men,
the rebel yell was a falsetto yelp which, when
heard at a distance, reminded one of a lot of
school boys at play. It was a peculiar affair for a
battle yell, but though we made fun of it at first,
we grew to respect it before the war was over.
When the Union men charged, it was heads
erect, shoulders squared and thrown back,
and with a firm stride. But when the Johnnies
charged, it was with a jog trot in a half-bent
position, and although they might be met with
heavy and blighting volleys, they came on with
the pertinacity of bulldogs, filling up the gaps
and trotting on with their never-ceasing "ki-yi"
until we found them face-to-face.[177]

—*Union soldier Gilbert Adam Hays*

My dear Edward: I have always been proud
of you, and since your connection with the
Confederate army, I have been prouder of
you than ever before. I would not have you do
anything wrong for the world, but before God,
Edward, unless you come home we must die.
Last night I was aroused by little Eddie's crying.
I called and said, "What is the matter, Eddie?"
and he said, "Oh, Mamma! I am so hungry."
And Lucy, Edward, your darling Lucy; she
never complains, but she is growing thinner
every day. And before God, Edward, unless you
come home, we must die. Your Mary.[178]

> —*Letter presented by Confederate deserter*
> *Edward Cooper in his defense at his*
> *court-martial*

Sitting at the base of a pine tree I saw a line
sergeant. His face was stained with blood, which
had oozed from under a bandage made of an old

shirtsleeve, tightly bound around his eyes. By
his side sat a little drummer boy, with unstrung
drum and the sticks put up standing on the
ground before him. The muscular form of the
sergeant was bent forward, his chin resting on his
hands, his elbows on his knees. His figure con-
veyed to me the impression of utter hopelessness.
The small drummer looked up the road, and
then down the road, with anxious gaze. I stopped
for an instant, and asked, "What is the matter?"
The drummer looked up at me, his blue eyes
filled with tears, and answered: "He's my father.
Both his eyes were blinded on the picket line this
morning. I am waiting for an ambulance to come
along. I don't know where the field hospitals
are." I hurriedly pointed in the direction of some
field hospitals we had passed a few hundred yards
back. The two rose up and walked slowly off, the
son leading his blinded father by the hand, leading him to the operating table, and I hastened
on, swallowing my tears.[179]

—*Union soldier Frank Wilkeson*

6

Facing the Inevitable

THE LEADERSHIP OF Robert E. Lee and Stonewall Jackson, combined with the valor of Southern troops, allowed the South to keep the war a virtual stalemate in Virginia for four years. Through the leadership of Ulysses S. Grant and William Tecumseh Sherman, and corresponding valor of Northern troops, the North was able to defeat Southern armies it faced in the western theater of the war and overrun virtually every Southern state east of the Mississippi River except Virginia. After Grant was brought east to face Lee, and Sherman marched all the way across Georgia virtually unopposed, most people saw the South's defeat as inevitable. What had begun four years earlier at Fort Sumter would end at the Appomattox Court House, Virginia.

★★★

My dear father, this is my last letter to you. I've been struck by a piece of shell, and my right shoulder is horribly mangled. I know that death is inevitable. I will die far from home, but I have friends here who are kind to me. May we meet again in heaven.[180]

—*Confederate soldier J. R. Montgomery*

Everyone knows and feels that we are fighting against hope itself—when everything is even now lost forever.[181]

—*Confederate soldier James Edward Hall*

Woe to those who began this war if they were not in bitter earnest.[182]

—*Southern diarist Mary Boykin Chesnut, after Atlanta fell*

Confederate President Jefferson Davis
"If the confederacy falls, there should be written on its tombstone, 'died of a theory.'"[183]

The will of God prevails. In great contests each party claims to act in accordance with the will of God. Both may be, and one must be, wrong. God cannot be for and against the same thing at the same time. In the present civil war it is quite possible that God's purpose is something different from the purpose of either party—and yet the human instrumentalities, working just as they do, are of the best adaptation to effect His purpose.[184]

—President Abraham Lincoln, in his
"Meditation on the Divine Will"

If we are to die, let us die like men.[185]

—Confederate General Patrick Cleburne

I am a tired man. Sometimes I think I am the tiredest man on earth.[186]

—President Abraham Lincoln

Let us cross over the river and rest under the shade of the trees.[187]

> —*Confederate General Stonewall Jackson's last words*

I have seen what Romancers call glorious war. I have seen it in all its phases. I have heard the booming of cannon and the more deadly rattle of musketry at a distance—I have heard it all nearby and been under its destructive showers. I have seen men and horses fall thick and flat around me. I have seen our own men bloody and frightened and flying before the enemy. I have seen them bravely charge the enemy's lines and heard the shout of triumph as they carried the position. I have heard the agonizing shrieks of the wounded and dying—I have passed over the battlefield and seen the mangled forms of men and horses in frightful abundance. Men without heads, without arms, and others

without legs. All this I have witnessed and
more, till my heart sickens; and war is not glorious as novelists would have us believe. It is only
when we are in the heat and flush of battle that
it is fascinating and interesting. It is only then
that we enjoy it. When we forget ourselves and
revel in the destruction we are dealing around
us. I am now ashamed of the feelings I had in
those hours of danger. The whistling bullets
and shells were music to me, I gloried in it—it
delighted and fascinated me—I feared not death
in any forms; but when the battle was won and
I visited the field a change came over me, I see
the horrors of war, but it was necessary.[188]

—*Confederate Major John Pelham*

Missus, we're even now; you sold all my
children; the Lord took all yours; not one left to
bury either of us; now I forgive you.[189]

—*An old slave mother, to her mistress, after a battle
in which the mistress's last son had been killed*

The enlisted men were exceeding accurate judges of the probable result which would ensue from any wound they saw. They had seen hundreds of soldiers wounded, and they had noticed that certain wounds always resulted fatally. They knew when they were fatally wounded, and after the shock of discovery had passed, they generally braced themselves and died in a manly manner. It was seldom that an American or Irish volunteer flunked in the presence of death.[190]

—*Union soldier Frank Wilkeson*

I beg to present to you, as a Christmas gift, the city of Savannah.[191]

—*Union General William Tecumseh Sherman, to President Lincoln*

I see the President almost every day… I see very plainly Abraham Lincoln's dark brown face with its deep-cut lines, the eyes always to me with a deep latent sadness in the expression… None of the artists or pictures has caught the deep, though subtle and indirect expression of this man's face. There is something else there. One of the great portrait painters of two or three centuries ago is needed.[192]

—*Walt Whitman*

The deep waters are closing over us.[193]

—*Southern diarist Mary Boykin Chesnut, after the Confederate loss at Nashville*

Fellow citizens, we cannot escape history. We of this Congress and this administration will be remembered in spite of ourselves. No personal significance or insignificance can spare one or another of us. The fiery trial through which we pass will light us down, in honor or dishonor, to the latest generation… We shall nobly save or meanly lose the last, best hope of earth. Other means may succeed; this could not fail. The way is plain, peaceful, generous, just—a way which, if followed, the world will forever applaud, and God must forever bless.[194]

—*President Abraham Lincoln*

I pledge to you that my study is to accomplish peace and honor at as small a cost to life and property as possible…and I will take infinitely more delight in curing the wounds made by war than by inflicting them.[195]

—*Union General William Tecumseh Sherman*

Our people are tired of war, feel themselves whipped, and will not fight. Our country is overrun, its military reserves are greatly diminished, while the enemy's military power and resources were never greater, and may be increased to any extent desired.[196]

> —*Confederate General Joseph E. Johnston, in April 1865*

I want no one punished. Treat them liberally all around. We want those people to return to their allegiance to the Union and submit to the laws.[197]

> —*President Abraham Lincoln, message to General Grant shortly before Lee surrendered*

Better a generation should die on the battlefield, that their children may grow up in liberty
and justice. Yes, our sons must die, their sons
must die. We give ours freely; they die to
redeem the very brothers that slay them; they
give their blood in expiation of this great sin.[198]

—*Abolitionist Harriet Beecher Stowe*

My shoes are gone; my clothes are almost
gone. I'm weary, I'm sick, I'm hungry. My
family have been killed or scattered. And I have
suffered all this for my country. I love my country… But if this war is ever over, I'll be damned
if I ever love another country![199]

—*A Confederate soldier*

Richmond has fallen, and I have no heart to write about it… They are too many for us. Everything lost in Richmond, even our archives. Blue-black is our horizon.[200]

—*Southern diarist Mary Boykin Chesnut*

General Sheridan says, "If the thing is pressed I think that Lee will surrender." Let the thing be pressed.[201]

—*President Abraham Lincoln, in a telegram to Ulysses S. Grant shortly before Appomattox*

There is nothing left but to go to General Grant; and I would rather die a thousand deaths.[202]

—*Confederate General Robert E. Lee, when he realized he must surrender*

We walked in softly and ranged ourselves quietly about the sides of the room, very much as people enter a sick chamber when they expect to find the patient dangerously ill.[203]

—Union General Horace Porter, describing the
surrender room at Appomattox Court House

I turned about; and there behind me, riding in between my two lines, appeared a command-ing form, superbly mounted, richly accoutered; of imposing bearing, noble countenance, with expression of deep sadness, overmastered by deeper strength. It is no other than Robert E. Lee! And seen by me for the first time within my own lines. I sat immovable, with a certain awe and admiration.[204]

—Union General Joshua Lawrence
Chamberlain, describing Lee's approach to
Appomattox Court House

To Honorable E. M. Stanton, Secretary of War:
General Lee surrendered the Army of
Northern Virginia this afternoon on terms
proposed by myself.[205]

> — *Union General Ulysses S. Grant, telegram,*
> *April 9, 1865*

7

We Are All Americans

CONFEDERATE GENERAL ROBERT E. Lee and his army, who had retreated from Richmond, were stopped by the forces of Ulysses S. Grant near Appomattox Court House on April 8, 1861.

Decisions made by the opposing commanders on April 9 had monumental benefits for the nation. First, Lee refused to heed the advice of Confederate General Edward Alexander, who suggested he disperse the Confederate army to continue fighting, guerrilla-style, rather than surrender. Lee knew what disastrous consequences such an action would have for "the country." Second, Grant's magnanimous terms of surrender permitted the Confederate soldiers to go home immediately, immune to future prosecution by government authorities. Grant had received this direction from Abraham Lincoln, who was by the end of the war undoubtedly the South's best friend. Tragically, within five days of Lee's surrender, Lincoln was assassinated at Ford's Theater in Washington, D.C.

Sunday April 9, 1865. Near Appomattox Court House, Va. Glory to God in the highest. Peace on Earth, good will to men! Thank God Lee has surrendered, and the war will soon end… I was never so happy in my life.[206]

—Union soldier Elisha Hunt Rhodes

The war is over. The rebels are our countrymen again.[207]

—Union General Ulysses S. Grant

Confederate General Robert E. Lee
"In the good providence of God apparent failure
often proves a blessing... My trust is in the mercy
and wisdom of a kind Providence, who ordereth
all things for our good."[208]

We have fought this fight as long as, and as
well as, we know how. We have been defeated.
For us, as a Christian people, there is now
but one course to pursue. We must accept the
situation. These men must go home and plant
a crop, and we must proceed to build up our
country on a new basis.[209]

> —*Confederate General Robert E. Lee, to*
> *General Edward Alexander the day of surrender*

The road was packed by standing troops as he
[General Lee] approached, the men with hats
off, heads and hearts bowed down. As he passed
they raised their heads and looked upon him
with swimming eyes. Those who could find
voice said good-bye, and those who could not
speak, and were near, passed their hands gently
over the sides of Traveller [Lee's horse].[210]

> —*Confederate General James Longstreet, after*
> *Lee's surrender*

On they come [the surrendering Confederate troops] with the old swinging route step and swaying battle flags. Before us, in proud humiliation, stood the embodiment of manhood. Thin, worn and famished, but erect and with eyes looking level into ours. Waking memories that bound us together as no other bond. Was not such manhood to be welcomed back into the Union so tested and assured? On our part not a sound of trumpet more, nor roll of drum; not a cheer, nor word, nor whisper of vain glorying, nor motion of man. But an awed stillness rather and breath holding, as if it were the passing of the dead.[211]

> —*Union General Joshua Lawrence*
> *Chamberlain, describing the surrender*
> *ceremony at Appomattox*

One of the Knightliest soldiers of the Federal army, General Joshua L. Chamberlain of Maine, who afterward served with distinction as governor of his State, called his troops into line, and as my men marched in front of them, the veterans in blue gave a soldierly salute to those vanquished heroes—a token of respect from Americans to Americans, a final and fitting tribute from Northern to Southern chivalry.[212]

> —*Confederate General John Brown Gordon,*
> *writing of the surrender at Appomattox*

We have shared the incommunicable experience of war. We felt, we still feel, the passion of life to its top. In our youths, our hearts were touched by fire.[213]

> —*Oliver Wendell Holmes*

At the sound of [the Union troops'] machine-
like snap of arms, General Gordon started,
caught in a moment its significance, and
instantly assumed the finest attitude of a soldier. He wheeled his horse, facing me, touching him gently with a spur, so that the animal
slightly reared, and, as he wheeled, horse and
rider made one motion, the horse's head swung
down with a graceful bow, and General Gordon
dropped his sword point to his toe in salutation.
By word of mouth the general sent back orders
to the rear that his own troops take the same
position of the manual in the march past as did
our line. That was done, and a truly imposing
sight was the mutual salutation and farewell.[214]

>   —*Union General Joshua Lawrence*
>   *Chamberlain, describing the Confederate*
>   *commander's reaction to the Union salutes*
>   *at Appomattox*

Sic semper tyrannis! The South is avenged![215]
>   —*Actor John Wilkes Booth, after shooting*
>   *Abraham Lincoln*

Now he belongs to the ages.[216]
>   —*Secretary of War Edwin Stanton, at*
>   *Lincoln's deathbed*

The South has lost its best friend.[217]
>   —*Union General Joshua Lawrence*
>   *Chamberlain, on the death of Lincoln*

Of all the men I ever met, he seemed to possess more of the elements of greatness and goodness than any other.[218]
>   —*Union General William Tecumseh Sherman,*
>   *speaking of Abraham Lincoln*

Had he [Lincoln] put the abolition of slavery before the salvation of the Union, he would have inevitably driven from him a powerful class of the American people and rendered resistance to rebellion impossible. Viewed from the genuine abolition ground, Mr. Lincoln seemed tardy, cold, dull, and indifferent; but measuring him by the sentiment of his country, a sentiment he was bound as a statesman to consult, he was swift, zealous, radical, and determined.[219]

>   —*Abolitionist and former slave*
>   *Frederick Douglass*

Lincoln, old Abe Lincoln, killed, murdered!... Why? By whom? It is simply maddening... I know this foul murder will bring down worse miseries on us.[220]

>   —*Southern diarist Mary Boykin Chesnut*

Strange (is it not?) that battles, martyrs, agonies, blood, even assassination should so condense—perhaps only really lastingly condense—a Nationality.[221]

—*Walt Whitman*

Southern newspaper articles of three or four years ago make me feel very old… We have lived a century of common life since then.[222]

—*Northern diarist George Templeton Strong, in 1865*

The pageant has passed. That day is over. But we linger, loath to think we shall see them no more together—these men, these horses, these colors afield.[223]

—*Union General Joshua Lawrence Chamberlain*

I have never on the field of battle sent you where I was unwilling to go myself, nor would I now advise you to a course which I felt myself unwilling to pursue. You have been good soldiers. You can be good citizens. Obey the laws, preserve your honor, and the government to which you have surrendered can afford to be and will be magnanimous.[224]

—*Confederate General Nathan Bedford Forrest*

America has no North, no South, no East, no West. The sun rises over the hills and sets over the mountains, the compass just points up and down, and we can laugh now at the absurd notion of there being a North and a South. We are one and undivided.[225]

—*Confederate soldier Sam Watkins*

Madam, do not train up your children in hostility to the government of the United States. Remember, we are one country now. Dismiss from your mind all sectional feeling, and bring them up to be Americans.[226]

>   —*Confederate General Robert E. Lee, talking to*
>   *a woman after the war*

Neither slavery, nor involuntary servitude, except as a punishment for crime whereof the party shall have been duly convicted, shall exist within the United States, or any place subject to their jurisdiction.[227]

>   —*Thirteenth Amendment to the United*
>   *States Constitution*

I looked at my hands to see if I was the same
person. There was such a glory over everything.
The sun came up like gold through the trees, and
over the fields, and I felt like I was in heaven.[228]

> —*Former slave and abolitionist Harriet Tubman,*
> *upon reaching Northern soil for the first time*

How could we help but falling on our knees,
all of us together, and praying God to pity and
forgive us all![229]

> —*Union General Joshua Lawrence*
> *Chamberlain at Appomattox*

We are all Americans.[230]

> —*Ely S. Parker, Seneca Indian and member*
> *of Grant's staff, responding to Lee's comment*
> *that he was glad to see a "real" American*
> *at Appomattox*

Union General Ulysses S. Grant
"I felt like anything rather than rejoicing at the downfall of a foe who had fought so long and valiantly, and who had suffered so much for a cause, though that cause was, I believe, one of the worst for which a people ever fought, and one for which there was the least excuse."[231]

Excerpts from Jefferson Davis's Inaugural Address

February 18, 1861

GENTLEMEN OF THE Congress of the Confederate States of America, Friends, and Fellow Citizens:

Called to the difficult and responsible station of Chief Executive of the Provisional Government which you have instituted, I approach the discharge of the duties assigned to me with an humble distrust of my abilities, but with a sustaining confidence in the wisdom of those who are to guide and to aid me in the administration of public affairs, and an abiding faith in the virtue and patriotism of the people.

Looking forward to the speedy establishment of a permanent government to take the place of this, and which by its greater moral and physical power will be better able to combat with the many difficulties which arise from

the conflicting interests of separate nations, I
enter upon the duties of the office to which I
have been chosen with the hope that the beginning of our career as a Confederacy may not be
obstructed by hostile opposition to our enjoy-
ment of the separate existence and independence which we have asserted, and, with the
blessing of Providence, intend to maintain.
Our present condition, achieved in a manner
unprecedented in the history of nations, illus-
trates the American idea that governments rest
upon the consent of the governed, and that it
is the right of the people to alter or abolish governments whenever they become destructive of
the ends for which they were established.

The declared purpose of the compact of
Union from which we have withdrawn was "to
establish justice, insure domestic tranquility,
provide for the common defense, promote the
general welfare, and secure the blessing of liberty
to ourselves and our posterity;" and when, in
the judgment of the sovereign States now com-
posing this Confederacy, it had been perverted
from the purposes for which it was ordained,

and had ceased to answer the ends for which it was established, a peaceful appeal to the ballot box declared that so far as they were concerned, the government created by that compact should cease to exist. In this they merely asserted a right which the Declaration of Independence of 1776 had defined to be inalienable; of the time and occasion for its exercise, they, as sovereigns, were the final judges, each for itself. The impartial and enlightened verdict of mankind will vindicate the rectitude of our conduct, and He who knows the hearts of men will judge of the sincerity with which we labored to preserve the Government of our fathers in its spirit. The right solemnly proclaimed at the birth of the States, and which has been affirmed and reaffirmed in the bills of rights of States subsequently admitted into the Union of 1789, undeniably recognize in the people the power to resume the authority delegated for the purposes of government. Thus the sovereign States here represented proceeded to form this Confederacy, and it is by abuse of language that their act has been denominated a revolution. They formed a new alliance, but within each

State its government has remained, the rights of person and property have not been disturbed. The agent through whom they communicated with foreign nations is changed, but this does not necessarily interrupt their international relations.

Sustained by the consciousness that the transition from the former Union to the present Confederacy has not proceeded from a disregard on our part of just obligations, or any failure to perform every constitutional duty, moved by no interest or passion to invade the rights of others, anxious to cultivate peace and commerce with all nations, if we may not hope to avoid war, we may at least expect that posterity will acquit us of having needlessly engaged in it. Doubly justified by the absence of wrong on our part, and by wanton aggression on the part of others, there can be no cause to doubt that the courage and patriotism of the people of the Confederate States will be found equal to any measures of defense which honor and security may require...

...Through many years of controversy with our late associates, the Northern States, we have vainly endeavored to secure tranquility, and to obtain respect for the rights to which we were entitled. As a necessity, not a choice, we have resorted to the remedy of separation; and henceforth our energies must be directed to the conduct of our own affairs, and the perpetuity of the Confederacy which we have formed. If a just perception of mutual interest shall permit us peaceably to pursue our separate political career, my most earnest desire will have been fulfilled. But, if this be denied to us, and the integrity of our territory and jurisdiction be assailed, it will but remain for us, with firm resolve, to appeal to arms and invoke the blessings of Providence on a just cause…

…Actuated solely by the desire to preserve our own rights and promote our own welfare, the separation of the Confederate States has been marked by no aggression upon others and followed by no domestic convulsion…

…We have changed the constituent parts, but not the system of our Government. The Constitution formed by our fathers is that of these Confederate States, in their exposition of it, and in the judicial construction it has received, we have a light which reveals its true meaning…

It is joyous, in the midst of perilous times, to look around upon a people united in heart, where one purpose of high resolve animates and actuates the whole—where the sacrifices to be made are not weighed in the balance against honor and right and liberty and equality. Obstacles may retard, they cannot long prevent the progress of a movement sanctified by its justice, and sustained by a virtuous people. Reverently let us invoke the God of our fathers to guide and protect us in our efforts to perpetuate the principles which, by his blessing, they were able to vindicate, establish and transmit to their posterity, and with a continuance of His favor, ever gratefully acknowledged, we may hopefully look forward to success, to peace, and to prosperity.[232]

Excerpts from Abraham Lincoln's First Inaugural Address

March 4, 1861

FELLOW CITIZENS OF the United States:

In compliance with a custom as old as the Government itself, I appear before you to address you briefly and to take in your presence the oath prescribed by the Constitution of the United States to be taken by the President "before he enters on the execution of this office…"

…I hold that in contemplation of universal law and of the Constitution the Union of these States is perpetual. Perpetuity is implied, if not expressed, in the fundamental law of all national governments. It is safe to assert that no government proper ever had a provision in its organic law for its own termination.

Continue to execute all the express provisions of our National Constitution, and the Union will endure forever, it being impossible to destroy it except by some action not provided for in the instrument itself.

Again: If the United States be not a government proper, but an association of States in the nature of contract merely, can it, as a contract, be peaceably unmade by less than all the parties who made it? One party to a contract may violate it—break it, so to speak—but does it not require all to lawfully rescind it?…

…I therefore consider that in view of the Constitution and the laws the Union is unbroken, and to the extent of my ability, I shall take care, as the Constitution itself expressly enjoins upon me, that the laws of the Union be faithfully executed in all the States. Doing this I deem to be only a simple duty on my part, and I shall perform it so far as practicable unless my rightful masters, the American people, shall withhold the requisite means or in some authoritative manner direct the contrary. I trust this will not be regarded as a menace, but only as the declared purpose of the Union that it will constitutionally defend and maintain itself...

...If the minority will not acquiesce, the majority must, or the Government must cease. There is no other alternative, for continuing the Government is acquiescence on one side or the other. If a minority in such case will secede rather than acquiesce, they make a precedent which in turn will divide and ruin them, for a minority of their own will secede from them whenever a majority refuses to be controlled by such minority. For instance, why may not any portion of a new confederacy a year or two hence arbitrarily secede again, precisely as portions of the present Union now claim to secede from it? All who cherish disunion sentiments are now being educated to the exact temper of doing this...

...Plainly the central idea of secession is the essence of anarchy. A majority held in restraint by constitutional checks and limitations, and always changing easily with deliberate changes of popular opinions and sentiments, is the only true sovereign of a free people. Whoever rejects it does of necessity fly to anarchy or to despotism. Unanimity is impossible. The rule of a minority, as a permanent arrangement, is wholly inadmissible; so that, rejecting the majority principle, anarchy or despotism in some form is all that is left…

…Why should there not be a patient confidence in the ultimate justice of the people? Is there any better or equal hope in the world? In our present differences, is either party without faith of being in the right? If the Almighty Ruler of Nations, with His eternal truth and justice, be on your side of the North, or on yours of the South, that truth and that justice will surely prevail by the judgment of this great tribunal of the American people.

By the frame of the Government under which we live this same people have wisely given their public servants but little power for mischief, and have with equal wisdom provided for the return of that little to their own hands at very short intervals. While the people retain their virtue and vigilance no Administration by any extreme of wickedness or folly can very seriously injure the Government in the short space of four years.

My countrymen, one and all, think calmly and well upon this whole subject. Nothing valuable can be lost by taking time. If there be an object to hurry any of you in hot haste to a step which you would never take deliberately, that object will be frustrated by taking time; but no good object can be frustrated by it. Such of you as are now dissatisfied still have the old Constitution unimpaired, and, on the sensitive point, the laws of your own framing under it; while the new Administration will have no immediate power, if it would, to change either. If it were admitted that you who are dissatisfied hold the right side in the dispute, there still is no single good reason for precipitate action. Intelligence, patriotism, Christianity, and a firm reliance on Him who has never yet forsaken this favored land are still competent to adjust in the best way all our present difficulty.

In your hands, my dissatisfied fellow countrymen, and not in mine, is the momentous issue of civil war. The Government will not assail you. You can have no conflict without being yourselves the aggressors. You have no oath registered in heaven to destroy the Government, while I shall have the most solemn one to "preserve, protect, and defend it."

I am loath to close. We are not enemies, but friends. We must not be enemies. Though passion may have strained, it must not break our bonds of affection. The mystic chords of memory, stretching from every battlefield and patriot grave to every living heart and hearthstone all over this broad land, will yet swell the chorus of the Union, when again touched, as surely they will be, by the better angels of our nature.[233]

The Gettysburg Address: Abraham Lincoln

November 19, 1863

FOUR SCORE AND seven years ago our fathers brought forth on this continent, a new nation, conceived in Liberty, and dedicated to the proposition that all men are created equal.

Now we are engaged in a great civil war, testing whether that nation or any nation so conceived and so dedicated, can long endure. We are met on a great battlefield of that war. We have come to dedicate a portion of that field, as a final resting place for those who here gave their lives that that nation might live. It is altogether fitting and proper that we should do this.

But, in a larger sense, we cannot dedicate—we cannot consecrate—we cannot hallow—this ground. The brave men, living and dead, who struggled here, have consecrated it, far above our poor power to add or detract.

The world will little note, nor long remember what we say here, but it can never forget what they did here. It is for us the living, rather, to be dedicated here to the unfinished work which they who fought here have thus far so nobly advanced. It is rather for us to be here dedicated to the great task remaining before us—that from these honored dead we take increased devotion to that cause for which they gave the last full measure of devotion—that we here highly resolve that these dead shall not have died in vain—that this nation, under God, shall have a new birth of freedom—and that government of the people, by the people, for the people, shall not perish from the earth.[234]

Abraham Lincoln

Abraham Lincoln's Second Inaugural Address

March 4, 1865

*F*ELLOW COUNTRYMEN:

At this second appearing to take the oath of the Presidential office there is less occasion for an extended address than there was at the first. Then a statement somewhat in detail of a course to be pursued seemed fitting and proper. Now, at the expiration of four years, during which public declarations have been constantly called forth on every point and phase of the great contest which still absorbs the attention and engrosses the energies of the nation, little that is new could be presented. The progress of our arms, upon which all else chiefly depends, is as well known to the public as to myself, and it is, I trust, reasonably satisfactory and encouraging to all. With high hope for the future, no prediction in regard to it is ventured.

On the occasion corresponding to this four years ago all thoughts were anxiously directed to an impending civil war. All dreaded it, all sought to avert it. While the inaugural address was being delivered from this place, devoted altogether to saving the Union without war, insurgent agents were in the city seeking to destroy it without war—seeking to dissolve the Union and divide effects by negotiation. Both parties deprecated war, but one of them would make war rather than let the nation survive, and the other would accept war rather than let it perish, and the war came.

One-eighth of the whole population were colored slaves, not distributed generally over the Union, but localized in the Southern part of it. These slaves constituted a peculiar and powerful interest. All knew that this interest was somehow the cause of the war. To strengthen, perpetuate, and extend this interest was the object for which the insurgents would rend the Union even by war, while the Government claimed no right to do more than to restrict the territorial enlargement of it.

Neither party expected for the war the magnitude or the duration which it has already attained. Neither anticipated that the cause of the conflict might cease with or even before the conflict itself should cease. Each looked for an easier triumph, and a result less fundamental and astounding. Both read the same Bible and pray to the same God, and each invokes His aid against the other. It may seem strange that any men should dare to ask a just God's assistance in wringing their bread from the sweat of other men's faces, but let us judge not, that we be not judged. The prayers of both could not be answered. That of neither has been answered fully. The Almighty has His own purposes. "Woe unto the world because of offenses; for it must needs be that offenses come, but woe to that man by whom the offense cometh." If we shall suppose that American slavery is one of those offenses which, in the providence of God, must needs come, but which, having continued through His appointed time, He now wills to remove, and that He gives to both North and South this terrible war as the

woe due to those by whom the offense came,
shall we discern therein any departure from
those divine attributes which the believers in a
living God always ascribe to Him? Fondly do
we hope, fervently do we pray, that this mighty
scourge of war may speedily pass away. Yet, if
God wills that it continue until all the wealth
piled by the bondsman's two hundred and fifty
years of unrequited toil shall be sunk, and until
every drop of blood drawn with the lash shall
be paid by another drawn with the sword, as
was said three thousand years ago, so still it
must be said "the judgments of the Lord are
true and righteous altogether."

With malice toward none, with charity for
all, with firmness in the right as God gives us to
see the right, let us strive on to finish the work
we are in, to bind up the nation's wounds, to
care for him who shall have borne the battle and
for his widow and his orphan, to do all which
may achieve and cherish a just and lasting peace
among ourselves and with all nations.[235]

Grant's Terms of Surrender to Lee at Appomattox

April 9, 1865

*I*N ACCORDANCE WITH the substance of my letter to you of the 8th inst., I propose to receive the surrender of the Army of N. Va. on the following terms, to wit: Rolls of all the officers and men to be made in duplicate. One copy to be given to an officer designated by me, the other to be retained by such officer or officers as you may designate. The officers to give their individual paroles not to take up arms against the Government of the United States until properly exchanged, and each company or regimental commander sign a like parole for the men of their commands. The arms, artillery, and public property to be parked and stacked, and turned over to the officer appointed by me to receive them. This will not embrace the sidearms of the officers, nor their private horses or baggage. This done, each officer and man will be allowed to return to their homes, not to be disturbed by United States authority so long as they observe their paroles and the laws in force where they may reside.[236]

Farewell Address: General Robert E. Lee

April 10, 1865, General Order No. 9

AFTER FOUR YEARS of arduous service marked by unsurpassed courage and fortitude, the Army of Northern Virginia has been compelled to yield to overwhelming numbers and resources.

I need not tell the brave survivors of so many hard fought battles who have remained steadfast to the last that I have consented to this result from no distrust of them; but feeling that valor and devotion could accomplish nothing that would compensate for the loss that would have attended the continuance of the contest, I determined to avoid the useless sacrifice of those whose past services have endeared them to their Countrymen.

By the terms of the Agreement officers and men can return to their homes and remain there until exchanged.

You will take with you the satisfaction that
proceeds from the consciousness of duty faithfully performed, and I earnestly pray that a
Merciful God will extend to you his blessing
and protection.

With an unceasing admiration of your con-
stancy and devotion to your country and a
grateful remembrance of your kind and generous consideration for myself, I bid you all an
affectionate farewell.[237]

Endnotes

1. First Annual Message to Congress, 1861.
2. Before the antislavery society, 1842.
3. G. Ward, R. Burns, and K. Burns, *The Civil War: An Illustrated History* (New York: Knopf, 1992), 6. Hereafter *CWIH*.
4. *CWIH*, 12.
5. O. G. Villard, *John Brown 1800–1859: A Biography Fifty Years After* (Whitefish, MT: Kessinger Publishing, 2006), 461.
6. Dred Scott Decision, United States Supreme Court, March 1857.
7. Bradley E. Gernand, *A Virginia Village Goes to War: Falls Church During the Civil War* (Virginia Beach, VA: Donning Company, 2002), 18.
8. *CWIH*, 2.
9. Manisha Sinha, *The Counterrevolution of Slavery: Politics and Ideology in Antebellum South Carolina* (Chapel Hill, NC: University of North Carolina Press, 2000), 226.
10. *CWIH*, 9.
11. Villard, 563.
12. S. G. Hyslop and N. Kagan, *Eyewitness to the Civil War: The Complete History from Secession to Reconstruction* (Washington, DC: National Geographic Books, 2006), 23.

13. *American Whig Review*, Volumes 11–12 (New York: Wiley and Putnam, etc., 1850), 215.

14. Edmund Ruffin, *The Diary of Edmund Ruffin, Volume 1* (Baton Rouge: LSU Press, 1972), 386.

15. *CWIH*, 52.

16. James L. Abrahamson, *The Men of Secession and Civil War, 1859–1861* (Wilmington, DE: Scholarly Resources Inc., 2000), 3.

17. Rod Gragg, *A Commitment to Valor: A Unique Portrait of Robert E. Lee in His Own Words* (Nashville: Thomas Nelson, 2001), 27.

18. Eric H. Walther, *William Lowndes Yancey and the Coming of the Civil War* (Chapel Hill, NC: University of North Carolina Press, 2006), 222.

19. W. E. B. DuBois, *John Brown: A Biography* (Armonk, NY: M. E. Sharpe, Inc., 1997), 184.

20. *CWIH*, 5.

21. Rev. J. W. Jones, *Personal Reminiscences of General Robert E. Lee* (New York: Forge Books, 2003), 438.

22. Lloyd Lewis, *Sherman: Fighting Prophet* (Lincoln: University of Nebraska Press, 1993), 138.

23. Abrahamson, xv.

24. ibid.

25. A. M. Williams, *Sam Houston and the War of Independence in Texas* (Boston: Houghton, Mifflin, and Company, 1893), 354.

26. Allen C. Guelzo, *Fateful Lightning: A New History of the Civil War and Reconstruction* (Oxford: Oxford University Press, 2012), 205.

27. B. H. Liddel Hart, *Sherman: Soldier, Realist, American* (Cambridge, MA: Da Capo Press, 2009), 74.

28. Allan Peskin, *Garfield: A Biography* (Kent, OH: Kent State University Press, 1978), 86.

29. James M. McPherson, *Battle Cry of Freedom: The Civil War Era* (Oxford: Oxford University Press, 1988), 154–155.

30. Letter from L. W. Spratt to J. Perkins of Louisiana, who was helping form the Confederate Constitution. Printed in the *Charleston Mercury*, February 13, 1861.

31. *Macon, Georgia, Journal and Messenger*, Oct. 2, 1850.

32. David S. Heidler, *Pulling the Temple Down: The Fire-Eaters and the Destruction of the Union* (Mechanicsburg, PA: Stackpole Books, 1994), 42.

33. Abrahamson, 99.

34. To the cadets at the Virginia Military Institute, April 13, 1861.

35. *CWIH*, 24.

36. B. C. Miller, *John Bell Hood and the Fight for Civil War Memory* (Knoxville: University of Tennessee Press, 2010), 142.

37. *CWIH*, 8.

38. R. J. Rombauer, *The Union Cause in St. Louis in 1861: An Historical Sketch* (St. Louis: Press of Nixon-Jones Printing Co., 1909), 159.

39. *CWIH*, 14.

40. Harry E. Pratt, *Concerning Mr. Lincoln* (Springfield, IL: Abraham Lincoln Association, 1944), 52.

41. Herman Hattaway and Archer Jones, *How the North Won: A Military History of the Civil War* (Champaign, IL: University of Illinois Press, 1991), 19.

42. William C. Davis, *A Government of Our Own: The Making of the Confederacy* (New York: Free Press, 1994), 310.

43. Mary Boykin Miller Chesnut, *A Diary from Dixie* (New York: D. Appleton and Company, 1905), April 12, 1861.

44. Eba Anderson Lawton, *Major Robert Anderson and Fort Sumter, 1861* (Albany, NY: Knickerbocker Press, 1911), 17.

45. *CWIH*, 41.

46. Ford Risley, *Abolition and the Press: The Moral Struggle Against Slavery* (Evanston, IL: Northwestern University Press, 2008), 158.

47. Walter Edgar, *South Carolina: A History* (Columbia, SC: University of South Carolina Press, 1998), 355.

48. Time-Life Books editors. *First Manassas* (Alexandria, VA: Time-Life Books, 1997), 42.

49. Alan T. Nolan, *Lee Considered: General Robert E. Lee and Civil War History* (Chapel Hill, NC: University of North Carolina Press, 1996), 46.

50. Wilmer L. Jones, *Generals in Blue and Gray, Volume I, Lincoln's Generals* (Mechanicsburg, PA: Stackpole Books, 2006), 44.

51. *CWIH*, 55.

52. James M. McPherson, *Drawn with the Sword: Reflections on the American Civil War* (Oxford: Oxford University Press, 1996), 72.

53. *CWIH*, 82.

54. *CWIH*, 55.

55. James L. Roark, et. al., *The American Promise: A History of the United States, Volume 1: To 1877* (New York: St. Martin's Press, 2010), 514.

56. Andrew Hilen, *The Letters of Henry Wadsworth Longfellow, Volume 4* (Cambridge, MA: Belknap Press of Harvard University Press, 1972), 283–284.

57. Hyslop and Kagan, 207.

58. E. W. Davison and D. Foxx, *Nathan Bedford Forrest: In Search of the Enigma* (Gretna, LA: Pelican Publishing, 2007), 74.

59. Frederick M. Holland, *Frederick Douglass: The Colored Orator* (New York: Haskell House, 1969), 301.

60. Letter, Clara Barton to Steven Barton, May 19, 1861, Manuscript Division, Library of Congress.

61. T. J. Karamanski, *Rally 'Round the Flag: Chicago and the Civil War* (Lanham, MD: Rowman & Littlefield, 2006), 64.

62. Jeanie Attie, *Patriotic Toil: Northern Women and the American Civil War* (Ithaca, NY: Cornell University Press, 1998), 25.

63. Alexander H. Stephens, "Cornerstone Address, March 21, 1861." From *The Rebellion Record: A Diary of American Events with Documents, Narratives, Illustrative Incidents, Poetry, etc., Volume 1*, Frank Moore, ed. (New York: G. P. Putnam's Sons, 1862), 44–46.

64. *CWIH*, 55.

65. William J. Cooper, *Jefferson Davis, American* (New York: Random House, 2010), 367.

66. Jerry H. Maxwell, *The Perfect Lion: The Life and Death of Confederate Artillerist John Pelham* (Tuscaloosa, AL: University of Alabama Press, 2011), 61

67. Sarah Morgan Dawson, *A Confederate Girl's Diary* (New York: Houghton, Mifflin, and Company, 1913), 32.

68. *CWIH*, 55.

69. "Battle Hymn of the Republic."

70. J. T. Scharf, *History of Maryland, 1812–1900* (Baltimore: J. B. Piet & Co., 1879), 338.

71. "The Bonnie Blue Flag."

72. Sam R. Watkins, *Company Aytch: or, A Sideshow of the Big Show and Other Sketches* (New York: Plume Books, 1999), 29.

73. Douglas Southall Freeman, *Lee's Lieutenants: A Study in Command, Third Volume Abridged* (New York: Simon & Schuster, 2010), 462.

74. John Selby, *Stonewall Jackson as Military Commander* (New York: Barnes and Noble, Inc., 1968), 28.

75. *National Parks Magazine*, July–August 2000, 40.

76. John S. D. Eisenhower, *Agent of Destiny: The Life and Times of General Winfield Scott* (Norman, OK: University of Oklahoma Press, 1999), 372.

77. Iain C. Martin, *The Quotable American Civil War* (Guilford, CT: Lyons Press, 2008), 88.

78. Guelzo, 205.

79. Dawson, 25.

80. Larry J. Daniel, *Shiloh: The Battle That Changed the Civil War* (New York: Simon & Schuster, 2008), 249–250.

81. *CWIH*, 120.

82. Jean Edward Smith, *Grant* (New York: Simon & Schuster, 2001), 231.

83. Wayne Mahood, *General Wadsworth: The Life and Wars of Brevet General James S. Wadsworth* (Cambridge, MA: Da Capo Press, 2009), 213.

84. Carlton Mabee, *Sojourner Truth: Slave, Prophet, Legend* (New York: NYU Press, 1995), 173.

85. W. V. Iziar, *A Sketch of the War Record of the Edisto Rifles, 1861–1865* (Columbia, SC: The State Company, 1914), 70.

86. Alexander K. McClure, *Abraham Lincoln and Men of War-Times* (Philadelphia: Times Publishing, 1892), 196.

87. *CWIH*, 4.

88. Ulysses S. Grant, "The Battle of Shiloh," 1887. *Battles and Leaders of the Civil War, Volume 1*. R. U. Johnson and C. C. Buel, eds. (Norwalk, CT: Easton Press, 1990), 485–486.

89. Frederick Douglass, *Frederick Douglass: Selected Speeches and Writings* (Chicago: Chicago Review Press, 2000), 601.

90. *CWIH*, 82–83.

91. Shelby Foote, *The Civil War: A Narrative, Volume 1* (New York: Vintage Books, 1986), 471.

92. John B. Jones, *A Rebel War Clerk's War Diary at the Confederate States Capital, Volume I* (Philadelphia: J. B. Lippincott & Co., 1866), 318.

93. Joseph Wheelman, *Terrible Swift Sword: The Life of Philip H. Sheridan* (Cambridge, MA: Da Capo Press, 2012), 185.

94. Hyslop and Kagan, 179.

95. Louisa May Alcott and Kate Cumming, *Blue, Gray, and Red: Two Nurses' Views of the Civil War* (Tucson: Fireship Press, 2008), 16–17.

96. David G. Martin, *Gettysburg, July 1* (Cambridge, MA: Da Capo Press, 2003), 479.

97. M. J. Cosson, *Harriet Tubman* (Minneapolis: ABDO Publishing, 2008), 26.

98. John F. Marszalek, *Sherman: A Soldier's Passion for Order* (Carbondale, IL: Southern Illinois University Press, 2007), 261.

99. Ronald C. White Jr. *A. Lincoln: A Biography* (New York: Random House, 2009), 588.

100. Chesnut, Diary, June 9, 1862.

101. Rod Gragg, *A Commitment to Valor: A Unique Portrait of Robert E. Lee in His Own Words* (Kindle Locations 229–230). Kindle Edition.

102. Alcott and Cumming, 17.

103. William E. Barton, *The Life of Clara Barton: Founder of the American Red Cross* (New York: Houghton, Mifflin, and Company, 1922), Volume I, 110.

104. Benson Bobrick, *Master of War: The Life of General George H. Thomas* (New York: Simon & Schuster, 2009), 155.

105. Peter S. Carmichael, *The Last Generation: Young Virginians in Peace, War, and Reunion* (Chapel Hill, NC: University of North Carolina Press, 2005), 174.

106. Randall Bedwell, *Brink of Destruction: A Quotable History of the Civil War* (Nashville: Cumberland House Publishing, 1999), 169.

107. Martin, 112.

108. Bruce Levine, *Confederate Emancipation: Southern Plans to Free and Arm Slaves During the Civil War* (Oxford: Oxford University Press, 2005), 81.

109. F. B. Carpenter, *The Inner Life of Abraham Lincoln: Six Months at the White House* (Lincoln: University of Nebraska Press, 1995), 282.

110. Selby, 25–26.

111. Jennings Cropper Wise, *The Long Arm of Lee: The History of the Artillery of the Army of Northern Virginia, Volume 1: Bull Run to Fredericksburg* (Lincoln: University of Nebraska Press, 1991), 106.

112. R. A. Baumgartner and L. M. Strayer. *Echoes of Battle: The Struggle for Chattanooga: An Illustrated Collection of Union and Confederate Narratives* (Huntington, WV: Blue Acorn Press, 1996), 91.

113. *The Rebellion Record: A Diary*, Volume I, 81.

114. United States War Department. *The War of the Rebellion: A Compilation of the Official Records of the Union and Confederate Armies, Series I, Volume 38, Part 1* (Washington, DC: Government Printing Office, 1891), 226.

115. Michael Burlingame, *An Oral History of Abraham Lincoln: John G. Nicolay's Interviews and Essays* (Carbondale, IL: Southern Illinois University Press, 1996), 54–55.

116. *CWIH*, 138.

117. Campbell Family Papers, 1860–1886. P 900150. South Carolina Department Archives and History, Columbia, SC.

118. Jean M. Humez, *Harriet Tubman: The Life and Life Stories* (Madison: University of Wisconsin Press, 2006), 183.

119. Emerson's Journal, January 17, 1862.

120. Alcott and Cumming, 19.

121. James I. Robertson, *Soldiers Blue and Gray* (Columbia, SC: University of South Carolina Press, 1998), 48.

122. Joshua Lawrence Chamberlain, *The Passing of the Armies: An Account of the Final Campaign of the Army of the Potomac* (Lincoln: University of Nebraska Press, 1915), 22.

123. Gragg, 44.

124. Michael Burlingame, *Abraham Lincoln: A Life* (Baltimore: Johns Hopkins University Press, 2008), 685.

125. Wendell Phillips, *Speeches, Lectures, and Letters* (Boston: Lee and Shepard, 1872), 553.

126. Edwin S. Redkey, *A Grand Army of Black Men: Letters from African-American Soldiers in the Union Army 1861–1865* (Cambridge: Cambridge University Press, 1992), 48.

127. Richard Striner, *Father Abraham: Lincoln's Relentless Struggle to End Slavery* (Oxford: Oxford University Press, 2006), 63.

128. Rose O'Neal Greenhow, *My Imprisonment and the First Year of Abolition Rule in Washington* (London: R. Bentley, 1863), 352.

129. Kirby McCord, *Cemetery Ridge* (Langley, British Columbia: BeWrite Books, 2012). Clara Barton letter to her father, 1861.

130. Lucas E. Morel, *Lincoln's Sacred Effort: Defining Religion's Role in American Self-Government* (Lanham, MD: Lexington Books, 2000), 185.

131. Martin, 141.

132. Larry G. Eggleston, *Women in the Civil War: Extraordinary Stories of Soldiers, Spies, Nurses, Doctors, Crusaders, and Others* (Jefferson, NC: McFarland & Company, 2003), 174.

133. *CWIH*, 158.

134. Lloyd Lewis, *Sherman: Fighting Prophet* (Lincoln: University of Nebraska Press, 1993), 360.

135. Bob Blaisdell, *The Civil War: A Book of Quotations* (Mineola, NY: Dover Publications, 2004), 123.

136. *CWIH*, 322.

137. Guelzo, 236.

138. Timothy T. Isbell, *Shiloh and Corinth: Sentinels of Stone* (Jackson, MS: University Press of Mississippi, 2007), xiv.

139. *CWIH*, 144.

140. *The Rebellion Record: A Diary of American Events, Volume II*, 479.

141. J. William Jones, *Christ in Camp: or, Religion in Lee's Army* (Richmond, VA: B. F. Johnson & Co., 1887), 170.

142. Lawrence Lee Hewitt, *Lee and His Generals: Essays in Honor of T. Harry Williams* (Knoxville: University of Tennessee Press, 2012), 186.

143. Spencer C. Tucker, *The Civil War Naval Encyclopedia* (Santa Barbara, CA: ABC-CLIO, 2010), 422. Also quoted as "Damn the torpedoes! Full steam ahead!"

144. Thaddeus Stevens, *The Selected Papers of Thaddeus Stevens*, Beverly Wilson Palmer and Holly Byers Ochoa, eds. (Pittsburgh: University of Pittsburgh Press, 1997), 322.

145. Tully McCrea and Sara Isabelle McCrea, *Dear Belle: Letters from a Cadet and Officer to His Sweetheart, 1858–1865* (Middletown, CT: Wesleyan University Press, 1965), 156.

146. Marszalek, 477.

147. McPherson, *Battle Cry of Freedom*, 809.

148. G. B. McClellan, *The Civil War Papers of George B. McClellan: Selected Correspondence 1860–1865* (Cambridge, MA: Da Capo Press, 1992), 288.

149. Rufus R. Dawes and Alan T. Nolan, *A Full Blown Yankee of the Iron Brigade: Service with the Sixth*

Wisconsin Volunteers (Lincoln: University of Nebraska Press, 1890), 90.

150. Bedwell, 104.

151. Martin, 66.

152. Donald J. Meyers, *And the War Came: The Slavery Quarrel and the American Civil War* (New York: Algora Publishing, 2005), 133–134.

153. *Battles and Leaders of the Civil War, Volume 1*, 479.

154. Charles Edmond Vetter, *Sherman: Merchant of Terror, Advocate of Peace* (Gretna, LA: Pelican Publishing, 1992), 123.

155. Walter F. Beyer, *Deeds of Valor: How America's Heroes Won the Medal of Honor* (Detroit: Perrien-Keydel Company, 1901), 84.

156. Alexander Hunter, *Johnny Reb and Billy Yank* (New York: Neale Publishing, 1905), 316.

157. Douglas Southall Freeman, *Lee's Lieutenants: A Study in Command* (New York: Simon & Schuster, 2010), 665.

158. *CWIH*, 147.

159. Frank Wilkeson, *Recollections of a Private Soldier in the Army of the Potomac* (New York: G. P. Putnam's Sons, 1887), 83.

160. Edward G. Longacre, *The Man Behind the Guns: A Military Biography of General Henry J. Hunt, Commander of Artillery, Army of the Potomac* (Cambridge, MA: Da Capo Press, 2003), 116.

161. Bedwell, 88.

162. *CWIH*, 224.

163. R. B. Browne and L. A. Kreiser Jr., *The Civil War and Reconstruction* (Westport, CT: Greenwood Publishing Group, 2003), 10–11.

164. LaSalle Corbell Pickett, *Pickett and His Men* (Philadelphia: J. B. Lippincott & Co., 1913), 224–225.

165. Hart, 303.

166. Elizabeth Keckley, *Behind the Scenes; or, Thirty Years a Slave and Four Years in the White House* (Champaign, IL: University of Illinois Press, 1868), 97.

167. Mary Boykin Miller Chesnut, *Mary Chesnut's Civil War*, C. Vann Woodward, ed. (New Haven, CT: Yale University Press, 1981), 696.

168. Douglas Southall Freeman, *R. E. Lee, Volume II* (New York: Charles Scribner's Sons, 1934), 262.

169. Guelzo, 274.

170. Bell Irvin Wiley, *The Life of Billy Yank: The Common Soldier of the Union* (Baton Rouge: LSU Press, 2008), 161.

171. Chesnut, Diary, 157.

172. William T. Sherman, *The Memoirs of General W. T. Sherman* (Fairford, Gloucestershire: Echo Library, 2006), 320.

173. Guelzo, 270.

174. Bedwell, 126.

175. *CWIH*, 96.

176. Foote, Volume III, 203.

177. Gilbert Adams Hays, *Under the Red Patch: Story of the Sixty-Third Regiment, Pennsylvania Volunteers, 1861–1864* (Pittsburgh: Sixty-Third Pennsylvania Volunteers Regimental Association, 1908), 240–241.

178. Daniel W. Barefoot, *Let Us Die Like Brave Men: Behind the Dying Words of Confederate Warriors* (Winston-Salem, NC: John F. Blair, Publisher, 2005), 181.

179. Wilkeson, 175.

180. Bedwell, 228.

181. William Marvel, *Lee's Last Retreat: The Flight to Appomattox* (Chapel Hill, NC: University of North Carolina Press, 2002), 128.

182. *CWIH*, 41.

183. Jefferson Davis, *The Rise and Fall of the Confederate Government, Volume 1* (New York: D. Appleton and Company, 1881), 518.

184. Burlingame, *Abraham Lincoln: A Life,* 711.

185. L. L. Hewitt and A. W. Bergeron Jr., *Confederate Generals in the Western Theater, Volume 1* (Knoxville: University of Tennessee Press, 2010), 246.

186. *CWIH*, 360.

187. Mary Anna Jackson, *Life and Letters of General Thomas J. Jackson (Stonewall Jackson)* (New York: Harper & Brothers, 1892), 471.

188. Maxwell, 61.

189. *The Rebellion Record: A Diary, Volume VII*, 17.

190. Wilkeson, 206–207.

191. Noah Andre Trudeau, *Southern Storm: Sherman's March to the Sea* (New York: HarperCollins Publishers, 2009), 459.

192. Matthew Pinsker, *Lincoln's Sanctuary: Abraham Lincoln and the Soldier's Home* (Oxford: Oxford University Press, 2005), vii.

193. Chesnut and Van Woodward, 694.

194. Abraham Lincoln Association, *The Collected Works of Abraham Lincoln, Volume 4*, Roy P. Basler, Marion Dolores Pratt, and Lloyd A. Dunlap, eds. (New Brunswick, NJ: Rutgers University Press, 1953), 519.

195. Marszalek, 303.

196. John G. Barrett, *The Civil War in North Carolina* (Chapel Hill, NC: University of North Carolina Press, 1995), 379.

197. Doris Kearns Goodwin, *Team of Rivals: The Political Genius of Abraham Lincoln* (New York: Simon & Schuster, 2005), 713.

198. Harriet Beecher Stowe, *The Writings of Harriet Beecher Stowe, Volume IV* (New York: Houghton, Mifflin, and Company, 1896), 290.

199. Foote, Volume III, 913.

200. Chesnut, Diary, April 7, 1865.

201. Telegram from President Abraham Lincoln to General Ulysses S. Grant, April 7, 1865.

202. Edward Lee Childe, *Life and Campaigns of General Lee* (London: Chatto and Windus, 1875), 318.

203. C. B. Flood, *Grant's Final Victory: Ulysses S. Grant's Heroic Last Year* (Cambridge, MA: Da Capo Press, 2012), 155.

204. A. Noel Blakeman, *Personal Recollections of the War of the Rebellion, MOLLUS, Third Series* (New York: G. P. Putnam's Sons, 1907), 272.

205. United States War Department. *The War of the Rebellion: A Compilation of the Official Records of the Union and Confederate Armies, Series I, Volume 46, Part III* (Washington, DC: Government Printing Office, 1891), 663.

206. *CWIH*, 380.

207. McPherson, *Battle Cry of Freedom*, 850.

208. Martin, 209.

209. Charles Francis Adams, *Lee at Appomattox: And Other Papers* (New York: Houghton, Mifflin, and Company, 1902), 11.

210. James Longstreet, *From Manassas to Appomattox: Memoirs of the Civil War in America* (Philadelphia: J. B. Lippincott & Co., 1908), 190.

211. Chamberlain, 260.

212. John B. Gordon, *Reminiscences of the Civil War* (New York: Charles Scribner's Sons, 1904), 444.

213. *CWIH*, 394.

214. Gordon, 444.

215. William C. Edwards and Edward Steers Jr. *The Lincoln Assassination: The Evidence* (Champaign, IL: University of Illinois Press, 2009), 1014.

216. Thomas Reed Turner, *Beware the People Weeping: Public Opinion and the Assassination of Abraham Lincoln* (Baton Rouge: LSU Press, 1991), 63.

217. Chamberlain, 280.

218. *CWIH*, 364.

219. Waldo W. Braden, *Building the Myth: Selected Speeches Memorializing Abraham Lincoln* (Champaign: University of Illinois, 1990), 99.

220. Chesnut, Diary, 522.

221. Walt Whitman, *Complete Prose Works* (Philadelphia: David McKay Publications, 1891), 314.

222. Eric Foner, *Reconstruction: America's Unfinished Revolution, 1863–1877* (New York: HarperCollins Publishers, 2002), 34.

223. Chamberlain, 271.

224. Davison and Foxx, 405.

225. Watkins, 199.

226. C. B. Flood, *Lee: The Last Years* (New York: Houghton, Mifflin, and Company, 1998), 152.

227. The Thirteenth Amendment to the Constitution

of the United States, which passed the House of
Representatives on January 31, 1865.

228. Humez, 183.

229. Chamberlain, 265.

230. A. C. Parker, *The Life of General Ely S. Parker: Last
Grand Sachem of the Iroquois and General Grant's
Military Secretary* (Buffalo, NY: Buffalo Historical
Society, 1919), 133.

231. Ulysses S. Grant, *The Civil War Memoirs of Ulysses
S. Grant,* Brian M. Thomsen, ed. (Forge Books,
2002), 473.

232. http://jeffersondavis.rice.edu/

233. Basler, Volume 4, 263.

234. Basler, Volume 7, 23.

235. Basler, Volume 8, 333.

236. Jay Winik, *April 1865: The Month That Saved
America* (New York: HarperCollins Publishers,
2006), 186–187.

237. Winik, 194.

About the Editor

Gordon Leidner has been a lifelong student of the American Civil War. He is a member of the Board of Directors of the Abraham Lincoln Institute and maintains the popular history website www.greatamericanhistory.net. Through the Great American History website, he has provided numerous articles and free educational material about the American Civil War, Abraham Lincoln, and the American Revolution since 1996. Leidner lives near Annapolis, Maryland, with Jean, his wife of thirty-five years.

If you have enjoyed this book, please consider *Abraham Lincoln: Quotes, Quips, and Speeches* and *The Founding Fathers: Quotes, Quips, and Speeches*, also by Gordon Leidner.